PITTSBURGH THEOLOGICAL MONOGRAPH SERIES

General Editor
Dikran Y. Hadidian

16

MANIPULATED MAN

The Power of Man over Man,
its Risks and its Limits

MANIPULATED MAN

The Power of Man over Man, its Risks and its Limits

EUROPEAN STUDIES
Strasbourg, September 24-29, 1973

Edited by
CHARLES ROBERT

Translated by
C. P. FRANK

The Pickwick Press
Pittsburgh, Pennsylvania
1977

128
C 749 h -T

Library of Congress Cataloging in Publication Data

Congrès de moralistes européens, Strasbourg, 1973.
   Manipulated man.

   (Pittsburgh theological monograph series ; 16)
   Translation of L'Homme manipulé.
   Bibliography: p.
   1. Man--Congresses. 2. Ethics--Congresses.
I. Robert, Charles. II. Title. III. Series.
BD450.C6247 1973a   128   77-24330
ISBN 0-915138-21-2

CONTENTS

*Rationalis creatura excellentiori quodam modo
divinae providentiae subjacet, inquantum et
ipsa fit providentiae particeps, sibi ipsi et
aliis providens.*   Aquinas

Intelligent creatures are ranked under divine
Providence the more nobly because they take
part in Providence by their own providing for
themselves and others.

PREFACE

Here is the publication of the Acts of the congress of
European moralists who assembled at Strasbourg from the 24th
to the 29th of September 1973 in order to discuss the "Power
of man over man, its risks and its limits". Without wishing
to alter the general intentions of the leaders of the congress,
we have given the Acts a shorter title, "Manipulated man".

The burning question remains; it should be convincing
enough to look in the newspapers and witness the stir created
from two announcements made by scientists in July 1974; first,
Dr. Bevis of Great Britain revealed, though somewhat prematurely, that three infants were born in Europe as a result
of artificial methods of fertilization, causing hot debate
amongst specialists in the field; second, in the United States,
biologists urged their international colleagues to give up
experiments on bacteria resulting in the introduction of anti-
biotic-resistant viral strains into the world. This experi-

mentation has occasioned the establishment of its own morality, as the World Health Organization was also tempted to establish at its colloquium in Geneva, November, 1973.

Were we endowed with exceptional perspicacity in choosing the explosive theme of the power of man over man for the congress of Strasbourg? Not at all. We have been preceded and informed by some significant work.

At the Ciba-symposium held in London in 1963 under the title, "The man and his future",[1] eminent biologists of the time exposed the power which man would hold henceforth over man himself. Until this time, one had usually praised the power which man had gradually acquired over nature in order to survive; now man became capable of changing the biological make up of man. It is not that specialists discovered at that date a power formerly unknown to them; they rather began in revealing what utopias one could extract, what projects were already in a phase of execution, and last but not least, the inevitable toll, that is, a definite and inevitable experimentation on human beings, otherwise said as a manipulation of man. In the very midst of the symposium, some participants became excited and complained about the general focus thereof. What seemed to be missing to them was a coherent assembly of moral criteria which would have permitted discernment between tolerable and intolerable experiments and preliminary ascertainments of the type of man the new techniques would eventually produce. The atrocities of two wars had made certain biologists very sceptical.

------

[1] The texts were published under the title: "Ciba-symposium, Man and his future", London, 1963.

For the classical moralist, the announcement of such profound innovations carried a great blow to the traditional standards which supplied his concept of nature. This concept, which tells how a man perceives and intends to develop in him that which is reputed to be stable, became thus inconsistent and useless, not by the always debatable circuit of philosophical analysis, but in the name of exact science, which one does not resist.

Numerous Christian moralists quickly perceived this challenge by the events and since 1967, at Münster/W, the Societas ethica, the interdenominational association having its seat at Basel, chose for its theme of congress: "La capacité de manipulation de l'homme". Professor F. Vogel, director of the Institute of Anthropology and Human Genetics of the University of Heidelberg, was the principal informant there.[2] The ethical reflection on the materials which Dr. Vogel had furnished could not have been but a beginning. It was very necessary to realize that the moralists had just been taken unawares.

In 1971, at Bastad in Sweden, the Societas ethica submitted its subject by making it more specific: "Les implications éthiques des acquisitions biologiques et médicales". Some young specialists contributed the information, Professor E. von Weizsacker, biologist at the University of Heidelberg, and active member of the World Council of Churches, and Professor P. J. Thung, biologist of the University of Leiden in

---

[2]The lecture of Professor Vogel, "Ist mit einer Manipulierbarkeit auf dem Gebiet der Humangenetik zu rechnen? Können und dürfen wir Menschen züchten?" appeared in "Hippokrates-Stuttgart", 38, 1967, p. 640-650, and in "Zeitschrift für evangelische Ethik", 12, 1968, p. 157-173.

4

the Netherlands. Moralists were obliged to face the evidence: they were not yet ready to face such staggering utopias.[3]

In the same year, 1971, the review *Concilium* devoted its 65th fascicle to the subject of manipulation: there, one prospected the immense terrain and battled for clarifying the vocabulary.

In 1972, Italian moralists held their 4th congress at Ariccia on the theme "Manipolazione e futuro dell'uomo".

In 1973, the Cardinal Suenens International Center of Louvain, organized its 2nd International Congress of Sexuality on the theme: "Insémination artificielle et reproduction humaine", viewed from the angle of manipulation. This congress was immediately followed by the 15th colloquium of the Center, concerning "Perspectives nouvelles en matière reproduction humaine". Thanks to this theme, the information and analyses at Louvain have formed a coherent whole and standards of morality have been able to be proposed which depended, some on conformity to nature, others on personal relationship.

Therefore, this work was no longer necessary to redo in Strasbourg.

During the session at Louvain, Professor J. Férin, of the Faculty of Medicine of Louvain, wanted very much to have some moralists walk through some human genetics laboratories and thus give his assistants and researchers the opportunity to expose their mid-term expectations and also to express

[3]The lecture of Professor E. von Weiszaecker, "Ethische Probleme aus der Biologie", appeared in Zeitschrift für evangelische Ethik", 16, 1972, p. 150-157. See Ch. Robert, "Le congrès de la Societas ethica", Bastad, Suède, 31 May-4 June, 1971, in "Revue théologique de Louvain", 3, 1972, p. 228-231.

their moral hesitations. This team of geneticists gave the decisive shock to the German, Swiss, and French organizers of the congress of Strasbourg, who, at the time sought to limit the subject of the congress as much as possible.

Under the effect of this shock, one decided to enlarge the theme of the congress of Strasbourg instead of retaining it, with the intention of obtaining a provisory balance-sheet of what is said of the power of man over man by the researchers of different and often isolated disciplines.

The word "power" evidently evokes the significant analogies of manipulation of and experimentation on living man. It is, however, the most ample word, we have not believed it to be too ample, because a priori we wanted it to be free of all pejorative nuance. If it was necessary to define it, we would say that it designates the capacity which certain men acquire to make use of the technical means with which to intervene either in the biological programming of man, or, beyond this, in the pattern of his behavior, or finally into the world of his primary desires and without doubt into his thoughts.

The pace of the congress had been foreseen then in the following manner: Professor Férin, by an informative lecture on the developing expectations of artificial insemination and the transfer of human ova, was obliged to try, we do not make a secret of it, to produce at the congress the salutary shock which we had felt at Louvain: evidently it would be a question of an objective exposé, devoid of all oratory effect.

To enter into the game, then, we would want to accord to the other participants a double spontaneity; it is even indispensable if one wants to finish with even a partial balance-sheet in fundamental science. They needed total spontaneity in choosing the meaning given to the words "power" and "manipulation", then spontaneity in the employment of a method of analysis and reflexion on the material furnished by the sciences. We have gone just to the end of our concessions, in agreeing to establish a well-ordered program.

The motley of ideas which followed this appeared to us to be finally paying off; men raised in isolated disciplines and men of different scopes, were able to express themselves in front of us without casting a sidelong glance at their neighbor, and thus they have directly cured us of the deadly temptation which willingly lies in wait for the theologian and which consists of passing with impatience from fundamental research to the construction of security systems and from there to pastoral applications.

It is beneficial to restate that fundamental research is only situated as one of the articulations of ethical reflexion, it only constitutes a phase, but in making it of poor quality, one abandons ethics at the whim of opinion and publicity.

In spite of these reservations, a direction appeared gradually as the participants revealed their preparatory work: the power of man over man, above all if it is seen exclusively as manipulation, that is, "as a conscious and directive pattern, although hidden, of influencing man in the domain of social interaction",[4] unleashes an actual proliferation of ethical problems, which arise all along the theoretical and technical progress of the sciences which involve man.

From the session in the research laboratory, questions spring up: beyond what threshhold does experimentation on living man become intolerable? But also, what singular privi-

---

[4]The quite general definition which we suggest here is an extract from the lecture of Professor Rombach, published hereafter.

lege do the reproductive cells seem to enjoy in order to be declared untouchable in the laboratory for moral reasons? We have read these questions implicitly in the lesson of Professor Férin.

Next, the stage of the slow practical application of a technique to man, the interrogations are contradictory. When and in what measure to modify biological man, but on the other hand, if one refuses to touch his integrity, does one not deprive him of important chances to survive and live better? Is not risk always found in the origin of chance? Professor Férin has left it to the moralists to reply.

These questions will not find ethical response, as much as an image-model of man will not have merited the assent of a great number. The two German participants, Professors J. Illies, zoologist at the University of Giessen and Director of the Max-Plank-Institute at Schlitz in Hesse; and H. Rombach, philosopher at the University of Würzburg, researched the features of this image. The reflection of a personalist philosopher, Maurice Nédoncelle reveals another aspect.

It was astonishing that Mr. Illies, although he is a man of science, directed his attention toward that which to him appeared the most urgent, namely the end and not the means. Visibly seized by fear from his own foresight, he advised a steep ascent toward a personal liberty, which can only establish itself when going in the opposite direction of the biological slope of man. He sees here the only exit for escape from the apparition of masses of manipulated men.

Professor Rombach went further in the description of this liberty, the perfect image of man not manipulated: an apparent liberty takes for its operational mode a fabrication and exalts it until one wants to withdraw indefinitely the limits of power of man over man. The other liberty, that which preserves the image of man, constructs itself in personal creativity and offers the only antidote against the ascendancy of the power of man over man. Liberty of fabrication, or liberty of creativity, it is necessary to choose and this places very highly the ethical requirements of man remaining and becoming himself.

These two German participants have manifested a kinship of thought which must excite our attention: they both are anguished by the power which certain men have acquired over other men. They both, the philosopher and the scientist, called for a radical and personal asceticism, moral in essence.

The sociologist, M. J. Gritti, professor at the Catholic Institute in Paris, seized the power at another stage, that of communication. The applications of science would remain curiosities of laboratories, much as they often did in the seventeenth century, if the power of man over man was exercised in the form of publicity in the network of social communications: it consists of a subtle but effective enterprise of manipulation. Now that which Mr. Gritti said of this, finally gathers strength: according to him, all attempt of social manipulation comes to collision with a profound resistance in man, where all happens as if a law of supply and demand mitigates the effect of seduction. Certain listeners believed to be revealed in the solid depths of the individual, this first natural law which nobody, according to Saint Thomas, can tear out from the heart of man.[5] After the sociologist, we wanted to give the floor to a psychoanalyst, Roland Sublon.

---

[5] St. Thomas, *Somme théologique*, I-II, qu. 94, art. 6.

Then came two theologians: without previous consultation, they brought forward exactly the same preoccupation. A place where power is exerted by man over man, could it not be our Church where one teaches concrete norms, ready to put to action? That which these two lecturers advanced is by way of hypothesis of work, but also by virtue of great concern to consolidate the moral norm in distinguishing it more clearly from the law said to be judicial.[6]

M. J. Audinet, director of the High Institute of Pastoral Catechism in Paris, who was invited on the request of some German colleagues, posed in his lecture, "Strategy of Christian Ethic", the most pressing question of moral pedagogy: how to teach Christian ethic according to a specific pedagogy which the characteristic of all ethics imposes. Inasmuch as the moral imperative only calls upon submission, it resides outside of the ethical domain properly said; exactly in the troubled region of manipulation. The norm only becomes ethic in the attempt to convince. It draws its force, according to the "Declaration on liberty" of Vatican II, from the only truth.

Professor F. Böckle, of the University of Bonn, invited by some French colleagues, had come to Strasbourg, bringing some six extracts of theses, which continued the analysis undertaken by Mr. Audinet. He poses the following questions: from where comes the contents, concrete and immediately applicable of moral norms, which are said to be synthetic; comprising the norm given in the name of God and by the

---

[6]The subject had already been approached by J. M. Dièz-Alegria, "Manipulation et liberté dans l'Eglise", in *Concilium*, 65, 1971, p. 59-65.

Church? His response may surprise one: it always comes from a human experience made in a given cultural area and in a given epoch. What is the aim of all moral norms? Not at first obedience, but the good and the development of man interpollated by the norm, otherwise to say, humanization. What is the foremost quality of the verbal expression of the norm, precisely of that which must convince? Its transparence; in other words, a kind of evidence. What is then the rule which will permit men to discern that which is befitting to him? Mr. Böckle borrowed it from an article of Professor B. Schüller of the University of Bochum; it consists of the rule of preference, which makes one choose that which in such circumstances realizes the most elevated human good or evades the worst evil.

Recalled suddenly home on the eve of his lecture, Mr. Böckle charged Professor Korff, of the University of Tübingen, to present his six theses. One will find in these *Acts*, at the eighth lecture, the six statements of Mr. Böckle, each one followed by a commentary by Mr. Korff. The text which we publish has been reviewed by Mr. Böckle.

This time the analysis seems to reach the moral norm at its very root: passing in effect to the limit, Mr. Korff wonders if the contents of the norm were not provisory in all cases, and if only the aim or end of all norms, which is humanization, remains stable. Let us note that Montaigne, Pascal and Kant had already posed the ethical problem of content in these terms.

A conclusion as abrupt is always found strongly tempered by two facts: on one hand, it would be audacious in the employment of the rule of preference to situate oneself resolutely outside of ethical tradition, which is laid down in a culture, like a profound tablecloth, the experience of humanity; on the other hand, the individual cannot place himself with obstination outside of his community, the ethic having been placed in action, transmitted and learnt in a community; even if it requires personal assent, it is not an individual work.

That which comes from this difficult lesson, exposed with many nuances, is that a morality cannot present itself with a concrete and universal content without its taking account of the utmost end of the norm, which is the concrete good of the man called to follow it.

Cited in a thesis by Mr. Böckle, Professor B. Schüller intervened at the congress with the intention of avoiding a simplistic interpretation of the rule of preference, of which he seems to be the author. We are pleased to be able to publish this discussion here.

The specialists regarded the power which today man is capable of exercising over man: Mr. Férin outlined a moderate prospective. Mr. Illies, Mr. Rombach, and Mr. Nédoncelle applied themselves to tracing the profile of an image-model of the man who ought to survive. Mr. Gritti followed the enterprises of power in apparently harmless social relations and Mr. Sublon in the unconscious. Mr. Audinet, Mr. Böckle, and Mr. Korff sought to avoid the fact that a moral teaching places the accent exclusively on the contents of the norm and extends thus the aim, transforming it into judicial law.

We have wanted to sound a vast and difficult terrain only here and there; we have not been able to honestly design large reliefs. We are wary of systems built to function from a particular problem, because they collapse like houses of cards.

Practically, we have concentrated our efforts on two points:

1. Customs arrange themselves in their human stratum at first, as St. Thomas wills it: "The acts prescribed by divine law," he says, "possess a certitude not only because they are commanded, but yet because they are conformed to nature."[7]

It is in the first place there that it is necessary for us to see clearly to an epoch of change which makes of nature the creative reason and rather than the law of things, deduces the moral norm from the world of human relations.

The task which calls the Christian moralist, for the moment, consists less of establishing at each cry of alarm, "a provisional moral",[8] than bringing about passage of a "law of fear" to a "law of love".[9] Is it above all a question of pedagogy as Mr. Audinet insinuated? The years to come will tell.

2. Our two German colleagues, Mr. Illies and Mr. Rombach, intend to escape manipulation of man by a personal pedagogy of liberty. Will this be sufficient? We do not believe that they carried out their analysis thusly, for the simple reason that creative liberty by itself is not found yet in contradiction with manipulation, nor with the power of man over man in general. It is the fact in the very name of creative liberty that has released in humanity of today the enormous ascendancy of this power.

A creative liberty emptied of fixed landmarks appears to us to operate in an ambiguity all the more large, as the human power disposes of better focused techniques.

---

[7] St. Thomas, *Contra Gentiles*, LIII, ch. 129.

[8] Descartes, *Discours de la méthode*, 3rd part.

[9] St. Thomas, *Somme*, I-II, qu. 107, art. 1 and 2.

Today man looks to his morality for an elevated degree of security: jealous of his liberty, he will only submit to the norms which will appear transparent to him in the network of human relations which simultaneously supports and menaces him.

We would have been delighted to have furnished to our guests at the congress of Strasbourg a few sparse elements of reflection and research. For the moment it is too soon to place them in a good constructive project.

*

*   *

In the second part of the *Acts*, we published the work of groups which met in the afternoon; in a more precise way, it consists of some reports which have been read at the final session.

These reports are varied, therefore very significant. Some went thoroughly into one of the themes of the lectures of the morning, others added some aspects which we must have neglected, for example, that of the pastoral; others finally went beyond the methodological frame which we had traced and proposed for other congresses, some less fundamental research and we hope that the next European congress, announced for 1977 in Milan, is able to draw on these ideas.

The search which we have undertaken will continue in the years to come. Also we add here recent international documentation, which we do not claim to be exhaustive, but which gives some elements for further research. We thank Madame Marie Zimmermann for having it established according

to the method which she presented in her state thesis published in French under the title of "Documentation, ordina-
teur et communautés chrétiennes" and in English under that of
"Documentation, computer and Christian communities".

We hide nothing of the difficulty which certain members
of the congress felt with communication: in the Middle Ages,
we would have spoken Latin, in the 18th century, French, today
we find ourselves in a tower of Babel.

Since the end of September 1973, the date of the Strasbourg congress, massive phenomena, which one could call phenomena of the see-saw, have simultaneously confirmed our ap-
prehensions and surpassed our expectations: it concerns
social and cultural mutations, facilitated by a slow manipulation of minds.

The 25th and 26th of April, 1974, the German Bundestag,
by 247 votes to 233, introduced the liberalization of inter-
ruption of pregnancy during the first twelve weeks of pregnancy: a campaign of three years had preceded this vote,
which had permitted Christian Churches to put forth an im-
pressive series of arguments in opposition.

The 12th of May 1974, Italy, despite vehement exhorta-
tions of the Episcopacy, maintained the law authorizing
divorce by 59.1% for the whole country; and 68.1% for the
city of Rome.

The 28th of June 1974, the French National Assembly
rapidly and almost unanimously adopted a law extremely
facilitating distribution of contraceptives and the Senate
followed suit.

These profound changes do not surprise us; there will
be others. That which poses for us the fundamental moral
problem is the fragility of the barriers erected by the
official morality, by traditional culture, and in full

catastrophe, by the organization of the churches. It sufficed one blow of wind: the whole thing collapsed.

We, moral men, must therefore work hard to sort out
the immutable in mores in order to explain the norm of
humanization each time the unprecedented arises which generates the accrued power of man over man, in order to finally
communicate the entirety in a language which would be transparent today and which could be read by our contemporaries,
our brothers in the human community.

The organizers of the Congress of European Moralists of
Strasbourg 1973, warmly thank the Cerdic, who wanted very
much to incorporate the *Acts* in its own series of research
on institutional changes.

Charles Robert

PART ONE

Contributions to Research

CHAPTER I

Fertilization in Vitro
and Transfer of Ova

In manner of introduction, I believe it useful to describe to you briefly the initial stages of life. If we consider a standard menstrual cycle of 28 days, we may pinpoint
the moment of ovulation on the fourteenth day, which we consider as being day 0. Ideally, on days -1, -2, and -3, insemination must be accomplished; that is, the deposit of mas-
culine sexual cells in the feminine tractus. The sperm normally journey, therefore, a certain time prior to ovulation in
this feminine tractus in order to undergo certain transformations there which render them more apt to fertilize the ovum.
This is what we call the phenomenon of capitalization. Fertilization itself, that is, the meeting of the sperm and the
ovum, is accomplished on day 0 in the hours which follow
ovulation; one estimates that the time during which the ovum
is able to be fertilized is not more than 12 hours. One even
wonders if the fertilizations which occur toward the end of
this period of twelve hours, or with greater reason those
which occur even later, would not create some abnormal egg.
Fertilization takes place in the external third of the Fallo-
pian tube, and immediately the cell begins to divide. We have
at first an egg which shows but one cell, then after some
time two cells, then four cells, then eight cells, and then
sixteen cells. At this particular moment, the egg has the

appearance of a mulberry which embryologists call the morula.
During this phenomenon of cell division, the egg does not stay
immobile: it is transported toward the uterus, it journeys
therefore in the tube; the tubal transfer of the egg is accomplished thanks to the cooperative activity of the muscles of
the tube and the very long vibrating cilia which line many
cells of the tubal epithelium. This tubal voyage, this tubal
migration lasts approximately three days. At the end of these
three days the egg is in the morula stage, and contains between 16 and 32 cells.

It is at this particular moment that it finally penetrates into the uterine cavity. Here it floats freely in the
uterine secretions for approximately three days. It is the
period of free intra-uterine life of the egg. During this
period the shell which envelops the egg ("zona pellucida")
dissolves under the influence of the enzymes in the uterine
secretions. The dissolution of this shell prepares for an
important transformation of the egg. There is a formation of
a central cavity which contains some liquid. Very rapidly
the morula transforms into blastula (or blastocyst), which
presents itself in the form of a vesicle filled with liquid,
of a scale much larger than the morula; and in this liquid-
filled vesicle, the future embryo is represented by only a
few cells which one discovers at one of the extreme ends of
this vesicle. At the end of the seventh day, might one say
in order to add a little poetry to this exposé, the blastula,
for reasons which one is actually studying, feels the vital
need to draw near once more to the surface of the mucous
membrane which covers the interior of the uterine cavity
(endometrium), to attach itself and to embed itself into it
in order to find the abundance of nutritious material necessary for its survival. Until this time, the egg had found

the nutritious material necessary for its subsistance in the
liquids contained both in the tubes and in the uterus; but at
this moment of his development, that is the end of the sixth
day, at the dawn of the seventh day, its nutritious needs become too important and the egg must find a much richer source.
This is the reason for which, finally, this egg imbeds itself
in the mucous which covers the uterus. This is the beginning
of the capital phase of the nesting of the egg or of the implantation of the egg.

*
* *

All the stages that I just described very briefly to you
can be realized in vitro at this very moment. One may therefore achieve fecundation and the initial developments of the
egg in vitro. It is well understood that we do not have, at
least at present, the possibility of realizing an artificial
uterus. This is the reason for which that, once the egg attains a sufficient stage of development, when it attains the
morula stage, to 16 cells for example; or with greater reason
when it reaches the blastula stage, if one wants it to survive,
one is obligated to introduce it into a womb, into a uterus
adequately prepared to receive it. This is what we call the
transfer of the fertilized egg to the uterus.

What are the conditions which permit fertilization and
development of the egg in vitro?

The first thing is that we must obtain the necessary reproductive cells. We must first obtain the sperm, which is
no problem perhaps, sperm destined for fertilization in vitro:

either fresh sperm obtained by dint of masturbation, or sperm provided by a sperm bank. Sperm can be conserved for years, I think that the actual record approaches ten years. One may conserve these sperm at low temperature without their losing much of their capacity for fertilization. These sperm will have been treated in a special manner, that is the spermatozoids will be extracted from the plazma of the seminal fluid and from which one will make a suspension containing between 1 and 2 million of spermatozoids by cm3. Concerning the obtaining of the ovum, things are a little more complicated. One is interested, in fact, in order to increase the rate of success of fertilization in vitro, in using mature, or almost mature ovules, that is, the ovules which are found in a follicle ready to be released. This is the reason for which we are obliged to proceed following two different techniques: the first consists of choosing a woman whose cycles are regular enough and to follow the evolution of her ovarian phenomena, proceeding each day in providing the amount of hormones responsible for ovulation in the blood. This being done one may, thanks to other observations, sufficiently pinpoint the approach of ovulation. If this technique is unable to be realized, we may choose another. We may artificially start the maturation of the ovule in treating the subject, the patient, with some adequate dosage of gonadotropic hormones. This having been said, how may one recover the ovule? A little harmless surgical intervention is necessary. We must proceed to that which we call laparoscope, that is one makes a small incision the length of one centimeter near the navel, and that one introduces through there an apparatus which permits us: to see the ovaries, to study the situation of the follicle in which the rupture is about to take place, and to puncture this follicle and to pump out the ovule

23

situated therein. When the woman is prepared by the gonadotropins, one may eventually, in producing a certain sur-
charge of gonadotropins, obtain several mature or almost
mature follicles, which permits us to obtain not a single
ovum as is generally the case, but eventually 2, 3, or 4
simultaneously.

The ovules obtained thusly are placed in culture of a
special milieu and after several hours of incubation at an
adequate temperature, they are placed in the presence of
spermatozoids; the whole thing will be placed in an incuba-
tor for a certain time and one will regularly control the
result. This fertilization in vitro succeeds in a regular
manner with animal cells, and more precisely with certain
types: the mouse, the rabbit. Concerning the human type,
one has equally succeeded with fertilization in vitro and
one has obtained the development of the human egg until the
blastula stage, the blastula stage having been achieved
after about 150 hours of incubation. The problem at the
present day is the control of the quality and of the normal
character of the eggs obtained thusly. These studies bear
on the present day concerning a few dozen human eggs. As
much as one is able to judge, it seems that human eggs obtained thusly are not distinguished in any way from human
eggs recovered from the uterus and in the tubes. It seems
that their development is normal.

*
* *

I arrive now to the part of this exposé which interests
you directly. If biologists have wanted to conduct these

experiments and have succeeded with them, the question is to discover what purpose they serve. What does one propose to do with these human eggs? One may do many things.

In the minds of biologists, a portion of human eggs which will be obtained thusly will be destined to be sacrificed. For what reasons? First of all the method itself. It is evident that such a method supposes some losses; at first glance this might frighten one. However I must point out to you a fact which is often misunderstood. If we observe what happens in nature itself, in fertilization, in spontaneous pregnancy, we arrive at a conclusion which is valid for all animals as well as the human type, that about 30% of fertilized eggs disappear more or less rapidly after fertilization. These eggs may disappear before the embedding, or if they succeed in their uterine implantation, they disappear rapidly afterwards. More or less 30%, such is the natural squandering of the reproductive function on this point.

A second reason for which biologists will decide to sacrifice a certain number of these human eggs is for the fundamental study of the process of fertilization itself, the fundamental study of the first stages of life, also the study of the consequences of tardy fertilization, which might produce some serious malformations.

A third reason is to be able to study the eventual toxic effects of drugs on eggs. You know that at the present the administration of medication and of apparently inoffensive drugs to the pregnant woman poses very serious problems. It is extremely difficult, when one introduces to us a new medication, to know if it will be dangerous for the human egg or for the fetus in process of development. Of course, we might do animal experimentation; but it is necessary to underline the fact that there are considerable differences between one species and another in the matter of eventual toxicity of a medication with regard to an egg in the developmental process. We are not able, therefore, to avoid the necessary stage of experimentation on human beings.

A fourth reason for which biologists must sacrifice a certain number of human eggs, is due to the focus of a technique which would permit the correction of certain genetic anomalies by the injection into the egg of cells provided by another egg not carrying the genetic defects in question. Therefore this would be the introduction into an egg of cells originating from another individual. One may even go very far in this domain: one may accomplish the total fusion of two different eggs and,if this technique is applied to humans, fusion of two potentially different human beings. This kind of total fusion has been realized in the animal species; and I give you a striking example of what this may produce, if the fusion concerns eggs of opposite sexes, a male egg and a female egg. One will obtain in this case a hermaphrodite. Such are the different reasons for which the biologist will be practically obligated to sacrifice a certain number of human eggs.

What will they do with human eggs which will not be sacrificed and which will be destined to pursue normal evolution? For these eggs, it will be necessary at first to succeed in the transfer, that is in their introduction into the uterus, in such a way which allows their implantation and thus the pursuit of gestation. The transfer in question has been realized with success with animals: with a few hundred examples of mice and a few dozen examples of rabbits. At the present no attempt at a transfer has succeeded in the human species, but it is a question of months or at the most a year or two.

Fertilization in vitro, followed by transfer, interests doctors for the following reasons: first of all, for the treatment of certain feminine sterilities. With certain women, in fact, the tubes are blocked irretrievably; or even the tubes may be nonexistent, they have been taken out during prior interventions. In this case, we may take the husband's sperm, we may take the wife's ovule, succeed in the fertilization in vitro and transfer the egg to the uterus; all of which does not seem to pose great problems.

This technique might equally be used for women for which sterility depends on an ovarian fault (agenesis or dysgenesis), or a precocious menopause, or an ovariectomy. We may, in fact, use the husband's sperm, but we may have to call upon another woman in order to obtain some ovules.

Fertilization in vitro and the transfer will be equally useful for genetic reasons, when for example, the woman presents a great risk in the genetic design, she is the carrier of chromosomal aberrations. In this case, one will have two solutions: either one utilizes her ovules, practices fertilization in vitro and immediately afterwards one controls the chromosomes of the egg. If the chromosomes are proven to be normal, one proceeds with the transfer. If, on the contrary, it is not possible to obtain eggs with normal chromosomes from the ovules of these women, we still have the resource to call on a donor.

The same reasoning, the same technique may be used, when it is a question of a woman carrying genetic defects, again in these cases, if we use the husband's sperm, we will have to, on the other hand, resort to a donor in order to obtain some normal ovules.

One may also imagine wet nurses, who would be able not only to give their milk, but also to carry the infant from the moment of implantation until birth. These voluntary or mercenary wet nurses would permit certain couples to have genetic children in the case, for example, where the woman has submitted to the removal of the uterus (hysterectomy), or when the woman, for diverse reasons, is incapable of safely carrying the child. The same formula could be used when the woman has a serious illness which would be aggravated by a pregnancy. One may even imagine that certain women, for reasons of their occupation or simply of their egotism, would no longer accept carrying an infant and would leave this burden to wet nurses who would certainly be handsomely paid for this service.

These are a few of the perspectives in which the realization is very near; and I hope that this extremely brief exposé, which perhaps will raise a good many questions, will serve as a useful basis for your discussions in the fields of theology and ethics.

Dr. J. Férin

CHAPTER II

The Biological Limits
of a Possibility of Freedom

1) In the eye of the biologist, living beings are the substratum which permits the development of biological programmings. These programmings are essentially hereditary and provide for a certain margin of freedom for the process of apprenticeship in the single case of highly developed animals. This margin of freedom does not only say that there is already freedom for each individual animal; effectively, that the animal could not decide on which things to learn. At this stage, therefore, liberty signifies only this: being open to individual adaptations, exactly as the programmed computer is open to the storing of messages.

2) The input of biological programmings presupposes that sufficient stimuli enter into the game. They are in the domain of physiology what adequate motivations are in the domain of human will. The threshold of efficacity of these stimuli is variable; it can even be that in a conflict of instincts, or in the behavior of a child at play, this threshold has lowered to the point at which one believed to find present activities devoid of all finality. From the biological point of view, these activities have, nevertheless, a finality: the reestablishment of a normal state of tension.

3) However, a behavior which acted as though it was liberated of all constraint of biological programming, is only an inhibition with animals: in this case, in fact, a zone of programming is found to be blocked by the requirements of a superior zone. (Inhibition of nutrition, aggression, or sexuality, when there are simultaneously some requirements of a more elevated level.) A wolf which does not eat does not act freely; he acts with no liberty and he feels an evident malaise from this.

4) Any kind of anthropology which admits that man's background is his own biological programming, must reveal the human specific, that of being and that of acting, precisely there, where the will of the individual succeeds in seizing a margin of freedom from this programming. It is true that, even there, a zone of this programming may be found to be blocked, but this time not by some superior interests which would be strangers to the individual—it is by this interest of a higher order that is a proper motivation.

5) The field of tension which is born between this proper motivation and programming of this type, permits a discovery of a new dimension: the exclusively human dimension of morality. (Animals act in one manner: "analogically moral".) Moral conscience could not be interpreted as "internalized paternal authority" (Freud), since if it is only that, our acts, in their turn, would only be "moral analogically". Our liberty in view of moral acts (and at the same time, this acting itself), does not necessitate any proof of its existence, it must be experienced. (The natural sciences are founded upon the recognition and the comparison of experiences.)

6) However, there is also a way of experiencing the narrow limit of such a freedom; facing the powerful constraint

of biological programming. The dimension of freedom of morals must be constructed at the opposite of the slope which such a programming represents. This difficult enterprise may, in the different zones (and even in their totality) be made very difficult. In truth it may fail completely if the unfolding of different impulses has been perturbed either by repression, or by sublimation during the period of the development of the individual. It is above all in the precocious relationship, mother-child, which are found grave dangers of this kind. (Impulsive delinquents are precisely the men who do not succeed in their actions because of their deficient development. That is to say, they do not succeed in being a man, at least in different zones of impulse.)

7) In all facets of culture, a narrow network of laws and interdictions reflect the efforts undertaken by a given society for conquering a margin of liberty permitting human action; and this is done by obtaining a delimitation of the biological programming in a collective way (taboos). The ascesis is thus the indication of a culture in which one may trust. (The liberty manifests itself above all, at the beginning, in the liberty of being able to say no.) It is in this sense which the laws are valid in all the zones of impulse.

      a) Oral-Insidious Zone

         1. Nourishing prescriptions (in pure food, feasts)

         2. The delimitations of propriety (prescriptions for sacrifices)

      b) Zone of Intentionality (= the realm of relationships)

32

        1. The prohibition of talking (to women of the family)

        2. The prohibition of touching (taboos, sacred laws)

   c) Zone of Aggressions

        1. The rites of reconciliation (blood brothers, adoption, the meal of a hangman)

        2. The prohibitions of killing (animal totems, the members of a clan)

   d) Sexual Zone

        1. Laws relative to marriage (monogamy, exogamy, etc.)

        2. Sexual taboos (taboo of incest, impurity of women)

8) In the cultural movement of humanity, according to an identical continuation (identical to that of the appearance of these zones of impulse in the individual development), the virtual liberty--that which says no, because the saying of yes is only a particular case of no--frees itself, so to speak, from the demands of society and of its laws, and is thus entrusted to the individual himself, in view of the unfolding of his personal style of life. Consequently, insofar as the individual is capable of becoming his own legislator, he is liberated from the collective structure of support, which is "the law" when it rules biological programmings. Thus the ultimate finality of cultural development is revealed: the individual himself. His personality is characterized then by the freedom he has achieved despite the biological programming inherent in him.

9) A liberty of this kind remains forever menaced by personal frailty itself. An attachment, in the background, to powerful and highly personal contents, may very well liberate complementary forces, which aid the individual, in the course of his moral maturation, to grow "beyond himself", that is to say, beyond his biological programming. This relapse into these biological programmings is then felt as a weakness, like "sin". Moreover, the legitimate question bearing on the source of this force which allows one to elevate oneself above the biological level, cannot receive any biological response (that is to say, coming from natural science).

10) A freedom of this kind lives, moreover, always threatened by others. It is solely the respect of a freedom put into danger which can preserve it, whereas the putting to work by others of biological stimuli narrows the field of our freedom. Taken in this sense, seduction is a conscious intervention into the margin of liberty of others, by the reinforcement of biological constraints and their exploitation in order to serve the ends of the seducer (for example, the sexual releases in advertising; aggression in hateful excitement). For this reason, seduction is the opposite of love, because it steals freedom instead of giving it. In our relationships, we must respect the limit which the biological imposes on our freedom, in renouncing the exercise of a purely biological power. This is the fundamental law of love toward one's fellow-creatures.

11) Thus it becomes evident, why, from the theological point of view, God is love; it is that, in giving up power, He accords us freedom. In Genesis Chapter Three, this aspect of morality is evident. "The knowledge of good and evil" which man has just acquired, manifests itself clearly

34

as the *pleasure of seduction*. "Recognition that one is
naked" signifies to understand the functions of release of
one's own body with regard to another's. The reaction of
one's conscience to this discovery, that one possesses a
power on the freedom of another, is shame. It is not the
development of a biological programming which could be evil
(sin), but the fact of taking from another, by a conscious
and lustful excitation, this freedom which he acquired after
great efforts. (The oral factors of release precede the
sexual, even with the yahvist author: before even noticing
that she is naked--that is, that she possesses a power over
the freedom of her husband--Eve recognizes that "the apple
is agreeable to look at and would bring pleasure should it
be eaten". In sum, that the apple possesses a power over
the freedom of following the commandment.)

12) It is in the sexual life that most clearly appears
the worth of all the zones where stimuli do play. A man who
has recognized that his "nakedness"[1] is the agent of release
for the programming of another, and at the same time a factor
which limits the freedom of another, will never impose a
nakedness of this kind on another. On the contrary, he will
only accord a nakedness to another there where it no longer
threatens this freedom; that is in the mutual giving of that
which is the "being of one flesh" (which is of value for all
the zones of stimuli). This is why the fact of being naked
is felt to be shameful; all the direct factors of release in

---

[1]The double meaning of "to recognize oneself to be naked"
and "to have a view of the entirety of relationships" is still
fully contained in the primitive text of Genesis Chapter Three:
the Hebrew word "*erom*" equally signifies "naked" and "to be
cautious".

the zones of impulse are veiled (that is to say, pass in all
cultures for impolite, provocative, and offensive).

The intrusions in the biological programming of another,
which always signify a diminution of the chances of another's
freedom--now that the innocence in not knowing is lost--are
invariably the following:

Seduction: a conscious attempt, tending to steal psy-
chologically the freedom of another for egotistical ends; to
channel and to manipulate the needs of others.

Humiliation: the conscious demonstration of one's own
force and the power to dispose of the freedom of another in
order to demonstrate its weakness of the victim.

Joachim Illies

CHAPTER III

The Fundamental Human Question:
Self-Determination or Freedom of Man

I. SOCIAL MANIPULATION

Preliminary idea: by social manipulation we mean the conscious and controlled, albeit hidden, manner of influencing man in the domain of social interaction; in other words, it consists of the putting in place and the consolidation of styles of social behavior, with the intent of obtaining ends which have been determined, but remain hidden.

1. *The Phenomenon of Manipulation:*

The most well-known forms of manipulation are in the domain of publicity. Above all they are connected with the phenomenon of the mode, which is distinguished by the fact that some principles of forms introduced without motifs are accepted as general aesthetic principles after a short period. Of a still greater extent is the manipulation in *politics*, which makes it increasingly appear that almost all that it is possible to choose as a political goal may become the internal volition of a people (this is the problem of apparent democracies). Some analogous experiences are made in the domain of *culture*, where the "manufactured" is put more and more in evidence. *In general:* as an "old order of things" is gradually

38

abandoned, human nature reveals itself to be deprived of pre-
determinations, therefore vulnerable to manipulation of all
kinds and even desirous of letting itself be manipulated.

2. *The Philosophy of Manipulation:*

The comprehension which a man acquires of himself (in
psychology and sociology) is more and more fixed in specific
categories of manipulation. Anthropology, which commands
recognition today, is pregnant with manipulation. This appears in the interchanging utilization of the following categories: *socialization, internationalization, programming,
conditioning, mode of operation, "learning",* and *impregnation.*
To these categories correspond some fundamental science such
as cybernetics, information theory, systems theory, which
combined with psychology and sociology of manipulation form
a *human technology.* The example of Freud's theory of neuroses,
above all the Oedipus complex, permits one to discern the
underlying thesis: the interior of regulations coming from
the exterior (neurosis as "false belief").

3. *The Manipulated Existence:*

The phenomenon and the philosophy of manipulation combine
in order to form the global syndrome of the manipulated existence which is becoming the fundamental form of actual existence, as much besides that of the manipulated as that of he
who manipulates. The manipulated existence is born of the
technology of the interior world of man. Since the technology
and the manipulation combine, the world which is self-made is
on its way to completion: the unforeseeable perspectives of
the future, an absolute futurology, social utopias, a social

eudemonism. Everything is swallowed up into proper form for our time.--It is Marxism which, with greatest consequence, has adopted this form and has rendered fabrication absolute in the affirmation: "man makes himself". The theory of "the false conscience", which corresponds exactly to that "of the false belief" of Freud, shows it well.

The theory of neuroses and the critique of ideology reflect the self comprehension that man acquires today.

II. LIBERTY OF SELF-DETERMINATION

The problem: for a long time man himself took the aid of a model of manipulation (for example, the automaton of Descartes). It follows that he wanted to escape into "emancipation". *Emancipation*, that is to say, *self-determination*, is precisely the idea of freedom which a manipulated existence makes for itself. Manipulation and emancipation constitute the fundamental structure of the comprehension which man has of himself today. However the question remains, is man able to remove himself from manipulation by dint of manipulation?

1. *The Dialectic of Emancipation:*

The insufficiency of the twin manipulation-emancipation reveals itself in a dialectic impossible to surpass. Emancipation is not possible, whether received (an intuition of Kant) or if one gives it to oneself himself (an intuition of Schiller). That the idea of Emancipation is an entrance without exit finds demonstration in existentialism (the absurd of Sartre).

2. *The Structural Model of Freedom:*

Freedom is never born of self-determination, but it
springs from personal creation. To this effect, the "edification of the self" must remain foreign to the model of
fabrication and be rethought in a structural model. This
model shows that the edification of the self is a construction of the world and of the senses in different degrees of
success (this comes, one arrives there, this succeeds). It
is thus that one attains identification to that of the world,
to that of the self, to that of the senses; insofar as the
event, this process of identification is situated beyond the
alternative of doing, that is to say, of heteronomy and of
autonomy. A structural ethic is nothing other than the justification of this identification by creation.

3. *The Relationship with Creation:*

The idea of the creation of self does not oppose that
of the creation of the world. It is true that in order to
perceive it, it is necessary to take the concept of creation
in its genetic sense, that is to say, *structural*. The relationship of God to the world must no longer be defined as a
relationship of fabrication, but rather as a synthesis of
creations, that which requires certain modifications applied
to the classical concept of creation; however, they will not
bring us out of traditional teachings, but will make us pene-
trate more profoundly in its more intimate intention, and
will show that what actually happens in nature and in history
is integrated with the global process of creation.

III.   THE GRAND EPOCHS OF THE HISTORY OF FREEDOM

Preliminary idea: by structural notion of freedom we
understand a fundamental power. Man "exists", he "under-
stands" what it is to be. This comprehension holds fundamentally the sense of "the conscionsness (of self)". The
structural notion of freedom seizes the fundamental event
which is the being-man, and shows itself at three epochs
(fundamental history).

First Phase of Fundamental Power:

In order to be released from a situation of distress,
man has acquired in "a breakthrough" a power, which reveals
to him that his existence resists his environment. Man may
then celebrate, in the ecstatic forms, the event of the identification of his existence with his environment, of the individual with his community, of the life with its meaning
(prehistory and primitive history). It is the initial form
of "that goes" which is the acquisition of *necessity* and of
meaning.

Second Phase of Fundamental Power:

From this first stage of life, man is invested with a
new creation of the discovery of himself, of the "one arrives
there", found in worship and in art. In order to have access
to it, he should feel an exigency to a superior degree, which
he extracts as an "intense exigency" from freedom itself.
This origin is registered as a curve in a space of freedom
which is not preformed by a single event (superior culture).
In producing thus the dimension of that which is superior,

42

the creation of self engulfs all the other creations, which
have only subsistance for intention, on the level of simple
"work", even if the labor improbus (evil work) remains also
a creation of the self. The more the superior origin of
"art" becomes artificial (now the first form of power), the
more "work" appears external and not creative: the scissors
of fundamental power open brutally.

Third Phase of Fundamental Power:

It is no longer a question of the creation of values; we
are dealing with the creation of man by himself. Man reintro-
duces now the method of creation in his own existence whether
in the form of an individual development of himself, or in
that of a creation by group dynamics. This particular creation presupposes that the old "objective norms" have been
dissolved, not with the intent of destroying them, but in
order to reproduce them, thanks to the creation, under a form
bearing a distinct character.

4. *How Manipulation Came into Existence:*

Manipulated existence is born exactly in the gap between
the second and third phases of fundamental power (at the end
of the superior degrees of culture). The "elevated" demands
of culture are already satisfied, but the still higher requirements of "that which has succeeded" are not yet realized. Now
all appears possible. One may "do everything". The internal
laws of success have become invisible because one has rid oneself of the success as of one of the forms of the meaning of
existence. Henceforth, the success seems to depend only on

external givens, circumstances, and prerequisite "techniques".
The operational mode of fabrication effectively depends on the
form of the power "to succeed". One always forgets what are
the substructure and its type, in being content to think it to
be universal. In effect this model collides with things
which one cannot do by technology (the forms of society, the
foundations of the meaning, success). However, instead of
assigning limits to it, this model is exalted to the extent
of the exaggerated forms of a metatechnology without one being able to engender more than a crisis in constant progression. This crisis is ripe for a decision, as soon as the external technique is elevated to the level of the internal
technique and man begins to take his own nature into his hands
thanks to biology, medicine, psychology and sociology.

IV.   TRANSITION AND PERSPECTIVE

The problem: in what manner is the passing from the
dialectic of emancipation (that is to say, of the notion of a
manipulated freedom) to autogenesis of a proper creativity
(that is to say, the structural process of freedom) possible?

1. *The Praxis:*

It is not a question of finding a new concept of freedom,
rather it is in finding a new reality of freedom, of a new
"power to act". This reality can only emerge from its own
structure of progression. The real idea of freedom is not
acquired in the abstract in order to be subsequently "realized" artificially; it must be extracted of itself (by dint

of creation), it must be born of itself (incarnation of freedom). In order to bring it into the world, it requires all of history, even the current crisis. This engenderment by self does not tolerate any *revolution* by constraint, or any conceded freedom, but neither does it tolerate any *reforms* which would stall a world of ready-prepared freedom (*manipulation*). A freedom of creation only accommodates itself to a life which one prepares oneself. Because this life may rediscover itself in time in a few stages of the history of freedom, there is a place to admit a polychromy of historical existence, therefore a polymorphisin of cultural forms.

2. *From Manipulation to History:*

A genetics of manipulation and a sociological technique have perceived clearly that it is a question of new stages in the way of being men, however one was wrong, because one believed that thus one would be able to reach these stages by dint of fabrication, and one did not understand, that a behavior of fabrication would only voluntarily prolong an already unnatural stage.

The specific essence of man (the "nature" of man) cannot be artificial, it can only be created by each one. History is the continuation given to nature, with the help of proper means. But this demands the formation of a man, capable of engendering himself in a creative synthesis.

3. *Humanization of the World of Men:*

The actual endeavors of "humanization" and of "democratization" express this fundamental demand. This announces itself, for example, in the *reduction of art*, when skilled art is considered only as a preliminary exercise of the superior art of the creative synthesis of man. The same thing begins-- again in obscurity and sufficiently false--in *the reduction of morality* where there would no longer be a question of realizing values or precise norms; rather where it would con- sist of autogenesis of a world each time having new norms, in the process of realizing its identification with man. The "recognized value" would no longer be the real problem here, because it would have become a consequence which comes from itself. In an analogous way, it is the same with the reduc- tion of *religion*, which would no longer let man sojourn in a realm of adoration exterior to himself; it would take him along in the process of salvation that he would become active and operate a creative synthesis there. Analogous reductions are appearing in *philosophy*, in *the sciences*, in *politics*, in *social* and *economic life*. In these domains, the stake is existence and action in common within the social orders. It is from the structural point of departure which one gives them, that there is a way of seeing if these orders do not signify loss or subjectivation; it is at this point of de- parture that one finds the standard permitting one to dis- tinguish humanization of society from injustifiable reduction. The entry of man into the process of the Revelation, prepared and consecrated by the miracle of Pentecost, rendered possible and legitimate in the history of freedom, gives precisely meaning and content to the current crisis, which one will humanly surmount, in finding the Christian solution.

Heinrich Rombach

CHAPTER IV

The Manipulation of Minds

To be treated like an object? Such horror for a person! We are quite ready to protest when it is a question of our sentiments, but perhaps all the more when it is a question of our intelligence. We cannot admit that some consider it as docile clay between the hands of a potter without scruples. It is above all in this aspect that I would like to examine the threat of alienation which weighs on contemporary man.

Certainly, one could deny "a priori" that it is possible to manipulate persons. They elude your tricks as do the eternal beings. By sophism, barbiturates, or torture, one only reaches some of the cast-offs of society; the transcendence of judgment and the truth of its objects are inaccessible in and of themselves. A seducer or tyrant can only prevent the person from either appearing or subsisting on the social scene; or prevent the truth from being shown. The testimony they wish to extract, they cause to flee: they only gain possession of deranged puppets or the falsely incomprehensible. But this declaration, which has its price in metaphysics, authorizes no psychological or moral optimism; because it does not diminish the scandal, which is precisely that, as swiftly as possible, men have been able to dispose of the mind and the world of the mind, while pretending to maintain them and persuading other men that they do so.

The tragedy of manipulation is very real. However, for purposes of analysis, it is advisable to put it into proper context. Now the virtuous indignations are often confused. It would be preferable to oppose certain commonplaces in the subject matter. First, let us distinguish carefully from manipulation, the inhibitions of life in general. For example, the existence of pedestrian crossings and traffic lights does not violate me: I must respect them if I wish to drive in the city. A rule, more generally a legal order, and more generally still a supreme norm of thought or conduct informs my action without determining it. It is even an axiom of law that anarchy restrains us whereas the law frees us. It is an axiom of philosophy that freedom contains, by definition, reason. All which one may concede is that certain constraints or certain norms (and certain suppressions of constraints or certain suppressions of norms) may be used by manipulators.

Another error exists in the too narrow association of manipulation and direction. The phenomenologist in this respect must be very clear. Manipulation is only a perverted form of influence among human beings. The latter is very much larger and fundamental than the former. Now there is not influence without intersubjective causality and there is not causality exerted by one conscience on another without an imperative of contact, which always involves a good or bad effect, loyal or not to the causal orientation. That the effect could be salutary, that it is infallibly so in certain cases; even this is in principle nothing scandalous. To uphold the opposite is not only to make education incomprehensible, it is to annihilate all real relation amongst individuals and to deny the authority of perception. It is not for its power that manipulation must be reproached, it is its bad quality: its causality which enslaves instead of liberates.

The English philosopher, Austin, called "locution" the expressive development of speech; "illocution" the intention of the speaker who wishes to influence a listener; and "perlocution" the effect which results from this in the listener. He separates the three functions of language and in particular the second and the third, in remarking that, if one may say: "I want to convince you", one cannot say in all precision, "I convince you". Without entering into the meanderings of an argument, for my part, I refuse to accept this separation.[1] There is an effective reciprocity of right and action in the clear rapport among one conscience and other consciences, whatever may be the complexities of their connection.

These remarks will illuminate themselves in examining in succession the manipulator's point of view, the methods which he employs, the condition of the person manipulated and finally the serious problem of the possible battle against the degradation of the life of the individual by the molding of minds. We will leave to one side biological interventions, and to a certain extent, sociological interventions, in order to apply ourselves chiefly to interpsychological analysis. The reason for this being that other collaborators in this volume treat the two former points. It is irrelevant that the first point depends on the second and the second on the third; because ultimately it rests in the mind of the individual which originated the whole process which will in turn change

---

[1] Austin himself seems to have judged it approximately in a manuscript note which he wrote in 1958. See J. L. Austin, *How to do Things with Words*, ed. by J. O. Urmson, Oxford, 1971, p. 102.

other individuals, alone or in a group, in their psyche or in
their body.

I. THE MANIPULATOR

The educator aims to produce a free human being by making
him discover his vocation with respect to the truth. In doing
so, he imitates the will of the Creator, who makes us exist
through ourselves. But not being the Creator, he can only
awaken a person already in existence, although he is inarticu-
late and is still merely a potentiality. He gives him the
principle of liberation in order to introduce him gradually to
his power for independent thought. The growing child is the
perfect subject for this educational aim, but this aim is
found in many other domains than pedagogy; it invades the network of human dialogues, and supposes a dizzying alternation
of formative emissions and receptions. We have said above
that the conscience which influences another conscience imposes and asserts itself fatally. The conscience does this
sometimes by irrational ways, but it does so as well by use
of reason, which appears and reappears in the individuals
which it unites. Let us go further: even what a person pro-
poses, he accordingly seeks to impose it as a proposition
effectively on others; considering that they will respond in
some manner or other to the view which they shall hold of
this proposition.

In which qualities does the manipulator distinguish himself then from those we have just called educators? In that
he is unbiased at least in part about the personal develop-

ment of others and prescribes to them a mode of being which
is foreign to them. He no longer takes his stand on an interior practicality for others but on a model in which he
has broken adrift with regard to others. A discontinuity
establishes itself thus in intersubjective causality. Another rupture occurs, no longer this time between the manipulator and the manipulated, but between values which
really apply to the manipulated and the manipulated himself:
it is the rupture of the bond between the singularity of
others and the universality of their end. All this pro-
hibits communications to result in a communion.

One could be tempted to conclude from this that the manipulator holds other people in contempt. It is not always
true. There are at least three forms of manipulatory intention. In the first, one manipulates others with a real dis-
interest: one wants to console them, to help them to live,
but one chloroforms them and substitutes for their liberty
a desire which is not their own or which will not spawn
their own.

In the second form, one admits that others have a "quid
proprium" to be made to expand, but one exploits their poten-
tialities for an interest which does not include their own.
The slave was invited to cultivate his talents for the exclusive profit of the master. Thusly, Greco-Roman antiquity
ascribed to itself workers, men of letters, and doctors. The
contemporary world is not in arrears: it ascribes by the
same method partisans for its different ideologies. "You
are," will say the propagandist, "a naturally fascist soul,
or republican, maoist, etc. Convert to the system, expand
yourself in this ideology in which I instruct you in what is
true and what is your homeland." Religious propaganda is not
exempt from committing such abuse, it has rendered itself

guilty and it has even occasionally refined some schemes which the political world is content to copy afterwards.

The third form of manipulative design is more radical. It does not differentiate any longer amongst men, it levels them and makes them uniform: it removes their brain and transforms them into swine, as with Circe, or into robots, as with our mass media. It is the putting to death of minds. One may then define them all as systems of conditional reflexes which are fashioned in series after a simple enough model: at the utmost, there could no longer remain an allowance of the unforeseen.

In order to do this, the manipulator or the consortium of manipulators still, nevertheless, count on the natural, because artifice never totally eliminates a spontaneous foundation, and this foundation is obtained by instinct of imitation or by contagious sympathy. In order to maintain the progress of fundamental conformism in a good state, one may make use of a motor which is intimidation in all its degrees (from human respect to terror). One also makes use of a brake (which ostensibly stops from time to time in order to replace one method by another so as to operate a variation on the same theme). Thus, the precautions are taken: stability is assured, with a guarantee against residual fancies or the uncertainties of change. Already this introduces us to another order of considerations: that of the methods of the manipulator.

II. METHODS

Interpersonal influence accordingly respects or damages, as the case may be, truth on the one hand and someone else's personality. In manipulatory influence, the most simple way to distort the rights of truth is to hide a portion of it, not by pedagogical economy or desire of progressive revelation, but by positively deceiving the partner. This is the method of stubborn silence. This silence is the negative side of an operation in which the positive side corresponds to that which one names vulgarly "baloney". God knows if we are able to detect its contemporary use in forming the large national or international currents of opinion, in nearly all domains.

With regard to the subjects who are the recipients of such messages, manipulation will certainly take many forms. It will be hindering, in order to stiffle the birth of germs of reflexion; magnifying in order to license depersonalizing and degrading impulses; and persistent in order to maintain the level of lack of original thought already obtained.

The processes vary according to the ways of communication. On the whole, we can distinguish three well-defined ways of communication therein:

(1) First, there is face-to-face conversation, where one may talk in pairs or in a little group. The influence of the manipulator depends then on all the factors assumed in classifying psychologists and microsociologists: the glamour of the eloquent speaker; and the adolescent passion for the well-beloved, both have an evident role here. In a situation of this kind, the projection of the personality reaches the others in an immediate way, but the paralysis which it produces may be all the more formidable.

(2) There are also influences from a distance in which an historic form of incalculable import will have been the written word. As writing preceded printing, a culture developed which rendered mental manipulation more difficult. When one reads the text of a manuscript, one has the leisure to think (especially if it is a weighty tome); with greater reason when one respects it as did the monks of the Middle Ages, and that it is the only way to convey the contents. The effacing of the physical presence of the author; the stepping aside and anonymity which this produces are beneficial conditions more than obstacles for the reader.

Things are changed due to the arrival of printing. From that moment onward, the situation reverses itself and manipulation recovers its rights. This recovery becomes certain with the invention of the press. A natural divergence is due to the succession of transfers from one language to another and from one people to another. What aggravates the situation from this point is the powerful and protean role of money. It is money which, in the transmission of events and ideas, hurts the truth most seriously and risks perverting or suppressing the judgment of the reader.

(3) Printing seems now to be in its decline and audiovisual media communications constitute a new phase of operation. Certainly, neither the great amount of printed tirades nor the television ruin the judgment of *all* persons. Many succumb to them, however, due to the information, conferences and debates televised, who will deny that the danger of manipulation is greatly augmented. In fact the coldness of printed paper has disappeared and a new warm contact has established itself, as if we immediately recover the personal exchange between the speaker and us. We are invested at the same time with vision and hearing without any personal inter-

ference. We pass from a printed representation which necessitates a mental reconstruction to a perceptible presentation
which dispenses with mental reconstruction.

Now this immediacy is a trap. Indeed, manipulation finds
itself in these circumstances in the sense that it has with
jugglers: in the art of producing illusions. The nearness
of audiovisual images paradoxically implies an extreme distance between the speaker and the recipient, the more so the
announcer increasingly complicates the circuit of mediation
in obscuring the perception of things and people which he
evokes. In a word, the apparent presence dissimulates a real
absence. The technical conquest of space and time by tele-
communications is admirable, but it pays for itself very
dearly; and the criterion of this distance is the impossibility of dialogue. Even if one introduced into the circuit
a delegation of auditors analygous to the newspaper column
of letters to the editor, such an antidote would be ridicu-
lous. With our letters on our table, we are consigned to
the solitude of the all powerful orchestra of waves.

The more technology leads us from the primitive dialogue
and authenticates the televised spectacle in passing by the
linotype message, the more also manipulation may slip into
interhuman relations. It only slips into human relations
by dint of being invisible; it bestows an invulnerability on
the surface of the manipulator, because the sacralisation of
technology defends him against detection. The medium (the
word is present in "mass-media") has taken the place of the
divinities. It has all the qualities; it is the new idol.
Already when one enters into a cinema one believes one is
in a temple; since the television can be placed in a kitchen,
it encloses in its little window the two household gods of
the twentieth century, if not Jupiter himself.

The functional methods are derived from the structural methods and it is easy to extricate the laws. There are three which permit a maximum yield:

(1) Manipulation will be in direct proportion to the repetition of the contents: it is the origin of the "bludgeoning" of publicity.

(2) Manipulation will be directly proportional to the number of recipients and their local density: the "sumpatheia" is moreover as rapid and profound as the humans form clusters well crowded together.

(3) Manipulation will be inversely proportional to the quality of the message: if one aims at the stomach, one will have more success than with the brain.

III. THE MANIPULATED

All that we have just examined will enable us to avoid belaboring the account of the manipulated. The assault which he undergoes, if he was well-lead, renders him passive from the moment of the killing of his mind, and much more so afterwards. Evil is not only a contemporary phenomenon, but it has taken epidemic proportions and has become subtle. Formerly, one only underwent manipulation in limited and often exterior sectors; today manipulation easily traverses barriers of the private life. Formerly, as today, one underwent manipulation without knowing it. But today one believes that one knows it that is, that either one does not know it or believe it. Formerly, the manipulator was easily distinguished from the manipulated; today the manipulator utilizes such diverse tools and communications that he is taken in his own trap and enters

in turn the group of the manipulated. Who can outline the
exact boundary between wholesome and adulterated products
which our substance has ingested?

And yet, the person resists. He resists by access to
Utopian and infantile romanticism which has helped the
"civilized" world for some years, but of which the theorists
and victims have nothing positive and viable to offer us.
He resists also by doing analyses which permit knowledge of
the mechanics of communication, the chances of distorting
the truth during the transmission, the ways of making an impact on opinion. Any good student of an Institute of Psychology or a School of Journalism may be able to expose the
stages of spontaneous or desired falsification of events by
dint of their transmissions. He may be able even to account
for the source, the intermediaries, and receiver; to discern
the levels of the contents, the role of the modes of con-
veyance, in short the machinery of efficiency and the idea
of finalities. One may even place the givens in formulae
and make an information science.

A first lucidity may thus awaken in us. But it is turned
toward the outside. It is at bottom the most simple. Another
power of critical awareness is necessary, and much less fre-
quently used. It is that of the manipulated's view of himself. Everyone wants to change the universe instead of changing himself. The Cartesian moral would deplore this with good
reason. Without pretending to accomplish the imaginary task
of returning to zero, each one of us could try to comprehend
his pre-comprehension so as to remain faithful to ones most
profound "I" with its requirements of impartiality and universality. It is in the furrowed field of operations that, if
he is manipulated without knowing it, he may cease from being
the manipulator of himself and of others for his share of

method which depends on his perspective. Thus we are obliged
to discuss the problem of remedy next.

IV. THE THERAPY

The picture which has just been painted in the paragraphs
of this article may appear to be too black. However it is befitting to react against the superficiality with which manipulation is habitually treated. It is not enough to play the
martyr or to challenge a certain political regime to rid oneself of an evil which is rooted in human nature and which
raises a terrible metaphysical problem.

Evil is increased tenfold by moral feebleness, but I
leave to the moralists the burden of stigmatizing sin and
teaching the ways of virtue. I take my stand, as I announced
previously, with a philosophical point of view; I ascertain
that the demographic increase of humanity on the planet en-
tails the grouping of individuals. Does not the minimum order
required for survival in a society of millions of human beings
keep us from crossing the line which separates legitimate re-
straints from the most cynical manipulation? From the moment
we ask ourselves this agonizing question, we are obliged to
acknowledge the sign of frailty of the concrete personality.
It is not fortified by standardization of its alimentary,
erotic or superfluous needs. The culture which it wishes
(when it wishes one) is carried to it in the form of prefab-
ricated ideas which it may acquire hastily and without tears.
The tempo accelerates and reflexion diminishes save with some
specialists which are in charge of choosing or distributing

the manna before the people. The disproportion is then enormous between the imperatives of the collective order and the precariousness of "reeds" supposed to be "thinking". How can one avoid the disequilibrium of cultural values, the subduing of subjective consciences and the triumph of lies?

One can do it only by a quest for quality. But what will determine and protect truth, beauty, and goodness? Whether we like it or not we are referred back to the responsibility of each conscience and the authority of a transcendent norm. It is a remedy for elites.

Its standard is qualitative purity. The pure logic of knowledge, such as we find it in the extent of mathematical thought and language, constitutes a remarkable cure for inferior passions and its essence escapes manipulation (when even technology would not escape it). There is an analagous purity in the order of sentiments: the radiance of the artist proves it; nobler still is the radiance of the saint. These qualities are worth more by virtue of their personalizing over those of pure thought. All are, in spite of the anonymity of objective expression, emanations from one person and carry the personal mark, but a bonus returns to whom rises in the meeting of vocations and the working together of consciences committed to the universal Word. We are then in the right to believe experimentally that we have passed the zone of manipulation and its ideologies. At the summit of the experience, the grandeur of spiritual genius is the power to elevate to that level those who are not able to do so by themselves. There is a fruitfulness here which is only produced in the intersection of views and in the admission of an absolute value.

Nevertheless, the solution remains sporadic and the ladder does not have a guardrail. The safety of a few leaves

us trembling before the ruin of a greater number. Some of
the elect are saved by dint of their interior route. Are
they also saved by their collective belonging? Again, we
run into tragic difficulties, the refusal to want the best
and above all, the inability to see it in order to desire it.
We have enough light for the personal progress of our person-
alities, we have not enough to preserve them from the will of
power which uses them and which they employ in worldly
society.

Is this to say that, excepting private wisdom and
qualitative standards, we do not have any means to reveal
manipulations and to destroy them without manufacturing
others to replace them.

This would be outlandish to maintain. There are cer-
tainties in the long run, which are convincing: there are
others which are indirect and relative but which one cannot
overlook. For example, when the molding of minds is unreason-
able, truth and conscience revenge themselves, contradictory
tensions separate from the group and cause a revolt. However
the decadence may also take a torpid aspect: mystified persons no longer plunge into an earthly hell, they fall into a
sterile sleep. Caliban protests, Caliban approves, Caliban
sleeps and Ariel flies away.

In summary, the only conclusion to draw is that one may
not rescue minds collectively by dint of a short cut in treating persons as if they were objects. There is not realizable
universality without the patient labor of educational awakening; similarly, there is not personalizing finality without
universal aim. It is a perspective of fruitful work, but un-
limited, where each partner is worth a world, and does not
fill the world. The worst of manipulations would be to let

men believe that absolute victory is finalized in their
time without their going through it.

                              Maurice Nédoncelle

CHAPTER V

The Power of Man:
The Challenge by the Humanities

Reflection on the prodigious advances of the sciences of biology or genetics poses questions equally formidable and exciting--indeed fascinating--to philosophy as well as to moral theology. The powers over the human organism--to the point of an eventual fabrication--do they claim to be assumed (or mastered) by some regulating structures within the person and humanity?

It all happens as if biology communicated to morality something of its expansive and conquering spirit. The kingdom of organisms readily requests, through cordial understanding, a powerful republic of consciences. Calling them with confidence and sincerity to judgments and prospections, to discernments and inventions of moral wisdom, is very naturally the part of scientists devoted to the physical and biological world. The sciences which they practice see opening before them a constantly controllable field. This endless mastery exercises an incontestable fascination which holds on to power credited with a power comparable to those moving in a different domain. It becomes believable *probable*--we will explain about this last term soon--to stimulate generously the research of the moralists.

This same presupposition of operative power risks spreading into the sciences of man. Their galloping expansion, the over-multiplication of their disciplines, their passage from the empirical stage to a more rigorous stage of science by model (at least for the more advanced) seem to authorize turning back to them a similar question: that of their power, of their own operative might. I will have occasion to go in depth into this idea of *power*--since it is the subject of this study --but I must in all honesty announce my inclination: I will be more concerned with the anti-power of the sciences than with their power, more with the deflation of great moral problems than of their inflation. This depends on a preliminary given: the image of a frontal progress, of a teleological dynamism remains rather foreign to the current practice and problems of the sciences of man. The questions posed to the moralists will be more in reverse than forward, more subterranean than obvious, in sum, more *archaeological*.

Before entering into the heart of the matter, I must make the angle of attack more precise, the kind of pertinence more suitable for me. Two orientations are offered to the study.

1. The powers of the sciences of man over man: what could be the effects on man and society of an action interconnected with individual or social psychoanalysis; characterology and its tests; sociologies, their inquiries and surveys; diverse structural analyses, etc. It is a subject particularly tempting because it responds to the desire to understand a global discourse on humanities. To be more precise this global demand is related to the general presumption regarding the formidable powers of the interconnected human sciences. I invite you to resist the temptation to solicit this global discourse and for two reasons:

The first is in the realm of epistemology. This global discourse would be possible if the sciences of man were sufficiently interwoven, and if the researchers made use of interdisciplinary concepts, valid at the same time for covert disciplines. Now, in the current state of research, it is rare that valid concepts can be used by several sciences at the same time. The more often we deal with these borrowed expressions which, as they pass from a first to a second discipline, become metaphorical so to speak for the second discipline: for example consider the same concept of metaphor passing from rhetoric to psychoanalysis, or that of overdetermination when it is conveyed from psychoanalysis toward sociology.

The second reason concerns the cultural effect of the present over-multiplication in the human sciences. They are effectively capable of taking one another into perspective, of analysing and critizing themselves indefinitely. I can--as I have done--undertake a rhetorical and ideological analysis of the language used by some famous psychoanalyst. He, by interposed generations, may analyse my proposition as a conflict with the father and a fury of self-destruction, etc. The human sciences weave among them complex relationships which produce at the same time numerous cultural intersections, and endless suspicions. The global result would be rather that of an anti-power, of a generalized suspicion.

2. Therefore there remains a second more modest way pertinent to the part of the seeker obliged to choose a discipline and a methodology determined from the multitude of those which offer themselves to him. The powers of man over man, such as they may be analysed by scientific practice--my own scientific practice--namely: the structural analysis of ideologies as a department of a sociology of information. After all, I have the feeling that this particu-

lar practice has a sufficient amount of complicity with the proposed subject: the power of man over man.

My procedure will be regressive or, if one will, *archae-ological*. It will consist of scrutinizing the relationship between the two branches of the title of the session: power *of* and power *over*...man.

The more *of* will manifest itself, the more the *over* remains uncertain; the more the *of* will blur, the more the *over* will solidify. We will envisage in succession: 1. The alleged manipulation of man who would engender social communication. 2. The fascination of ideologies. 3. The *archaeological* constraint of cultural codes.

I

For the first part, let us look at the question of social communication in the alleged effects of manipulation exercised on man. Since the thirties, first and foremost in America, with the industrial West following, educators, men of the Church, magistrates and a good number of politicians were preoccupied, and still are, with the unfurling of the techniques of collective broadcasting: cinema, radio, television, newspapers, comic strips, picture books, phono-records, and songs, pictures and commercials. Propaganda and publicity, exchanging their attributes, appear to exercise a formidable manipulative power of man over man. Literary or popular expressions such as *brainwashing, mugging, gang rape* illustrate the obsession, if not the panic, of many observers and responsible people. Naturally one turned to the sociologists and psychologists in order to ask them for a scientific evaluation of the effects of manipulation. Taken for granted in the question, manipulation has become the first theory of mass communication, before the war, during the war, and immediately after the war up to the fifties.

The spectacle of nazi or fascist, or yet bolshevik propagandas--techniques of a commercial publicity so greatly repetitive with the help of intensive slogans gave substance to this presumption with respect to the powers of manipulation.

Brainwashing, propaganda and anti-propaganda of war, the necessity to restore the market after the war prolonged the strong appearances of manipulation.

A useful unilateral *schema*, that of Harold Laswell, gave a logical form to the presupposed in manipulative power.

Who? says what? by what medium? to whom? with what effects?[1]

In this *schema* the maximum strategic activity is based on the *who?*--the source or the transmitter--whereas the *to whom?*--the intended or the recipient--is directed to receptive passivity. Communication functions in a unilateral way and this type of tracing gives a good image of manipulation. This *schema* will find scientific guaranties from behavioral philosophies and from the study of reflexes according to Pavlov. The work of Serge Tchaikhotine, revealingly entitled:

---

[1]Harold D. Laswell, Naphan Leites, "The Structure and Function of Communication", in *Mass Communications*, Urbana, Ill., University of Illinois Press, 1960.

Gang Rape by Political Propaganda[2] remains the classic of this state of mind.

Before taking into account the important contradictions raised by subsequent scientific research, let us ascertain that the presupposition of manipulation still has a hard life in our times within certain milieus. A few years ago, curiosity or panic surrounding the rumor of the *invisible image* was proof of it: it would have sufficed to slip in among the 24 images per second of a film, a single one, for a commercial product, only one and invisible to the retina, in order that on leaving the room, the spectators would be led *en masse* toward the purchase of the product in question! Verification made, rumor bordered on a practical joke.

More seriously and customarily the credit accorded to the effect of public opinion polls or yet to the impact which political leaders make on television proves that presupposition runs rampant in the streets. Has not one said in a peremptory fashion that General de Gaulle gained his electoral victories thanks to television, as did Napoleon formerly, his battle victories thanks to artillery.

I mentioned the contradictions raised by more refined scientific research (since the 50's). First and foremost, the detection of feedback, that is to say the shock in return, the active shock from the receivers to the transmitters. This return through the game of success or failure by the rhythms of infatuation and of disenchantment of which the causes must be sought in the demand itself, active demand which is satisfied or frustrated.

---

[2] Last edition, Paris, N.R.F. Gallimard, 1952.

In feedback, the most marked aspect is the negative, called the boomerang effect according to a suggestive image. This boomerang effect--return to the sender--is produced when the true public demand is unknown to the transmitter. Let us take two examples: one in politics, one in publicity. At the time of the French referendum on Europe in the spring of 1971, the partisans of *yes* (majority in addition to a fraction of the opposition) reserved more than three-fifths the television time, whereas the partisans of *no*, or of abstention, were relegated to the remainder. This was a shock to naïvely egalitarian public opinion. Boomerang effect; failure relative to the referendum in spite of the greater number of hours of television time occupied by the partisans of *yes*.

On the commercial level, the first publicity concerning instant soup and coffee appealed to the woman in need of rest and to the feeling of expeditious ease: seated on a comfortable divan the housewife had only to let it happen. This ran counter to the demand of the woman of today who desires to see herself recognized in her vocation and her social functions. Boomerang effect; total failure, it will be necessary next to show that instant soup and coffee increase the activity and responsibility of women.

I pass rapidly on to two other contradictions: the discovery of the role of local leaders of opinion and of *primary groups* (habitat, work, leisure, etc.) which surround the user. Communication is thus filtered by these intermediary agents: contradicted by the leaders of opinion and the primary groups, communication remains without effect; passed on by these agents, it comes to rest in the immediate environment of the recipient. All the same the propaganda of revolutionary war or in contemporary China counts on this immediate environment; the militant base and small groups. Populations formerly colonized have been seen to pass along subversive information,

more surely than the holders of power and of the massive means
of information could impose theirs on them. These verifica-
tions have led researchers to talk of two stages in communication and to underline the importance of the intermediary stage.

All these new researches and all these contradictions led
to the placing in relief the active role of the demand and
therefore of the receiver: "It is clear," affirms the American sociologist Wilbur Schramm, "that in order to understand
the impact and effect of television on children, we must first
separate the unrealistic concept of that which television
'does to children' and substitute for it that which children
'make of television'."[3]

Instead of a unilateral *schema* of a communication which
comes from the active strategy of the transmitter to the pure
receptivity of the recipient, a more operative *schema* presides
over present research:

The request is correlative to the offer in constant interaction with it: the messages make a circuit from the demand to
the offer and from the offer to the demand; and the effects
bring about a circular, reciprocal causality. An example
particularly stimulating illustrates the active role of the
demand, in an historical situation where one expected it the
least. Two Italian sociologists, Franco Rositi and Giorgio
Galli, struck by the many similar structural traits (social,
economic) in the situation in the U.S.A. and in Germany in
the 30's, astonished that comparable infrastructures in the
two countries led to diametrically opposed political solutions,

---

[3]W. Schramm, J. Lyle, and E. Partier, *Television in the
Lives of Our Children*, Stanford, Stanford University Press,
1961, p. 169.

strove to scrutinize certain aspects of the unconscious
demand of a collective predisposition either to a *liberal*
solution of Roosevelt, or to the nazi solution with Hitler.

To this effect, they have drawn up a list of popularly
successful films in the 30's and made an inventory of the
themes of these films.

Here are a few results.[4]

CONTENTS	German films	American films
1. Problems of personal morals	2.6%	16.8%
2. Superior ideals	18.6%	8.6%
3. Military life	13.0%	4.0%
4. Happy end	35.7%	45.5%
5. Sad end	23.3%	7.1%
6. Possibility for the individual to control evil and unhappiness	16.9%	53.3%
7. Impossibility for the individual to control evil and unhappiness	14.2%	5.0%
8. Optimism in action	14.3%	47.1%
9. Optimism by evasion	50.8%	31.9%

[4]*Cultura di massa e comportamento collettivo*, Bologno,
Il Mulino, 1967, p. 256.

Let us add, in order to corroborate this active role of
the demand and this circular causality between the demand and
the offer, a characteristic factor of modern societies said
to be advanced: the multiplication and the specialization of
relationships between social partners. I have the public
powers as partners from one definite angle and let us view
the automobile firm of Citroën from a different angle. In
a less developed society possessions, power and knowledge
were centered in the same restricted milieu and conflicts
also: the press, called *fourth power*, could make or ruin
the ministers. Contrary to a greatly circulated prejudgment,
in a modern industrial society powers are dispersed in an
increasing specialization. General Motors may crush small
firms on its way, but it can do nothing against Ralph Nader,
modest disputing lawyer, who would become the star of dispute. In 1968, one Cecil King, *all powerful* (it was believed)
magnate of the British press, took Mr. Wilson to task violent-
ly in a major editorial published simultaneously in the *Daily
Mirror* and the *Sun*.[5] The result, this was not when Wilson
resigned--that was a year later and under different condi-
tions--but it was Cecil King who was dismissed by his own
board!

It is time to conclude this first part. If there is
manipulation, it is by corresponding to a collective demand.
If there is causality, this causality is circular. The power
of man is apparent, manifest, the power over man is very uncertain, all the more uncertain.

---

[5] Olivier Burgelin, *La Communication de Masse*, Paris,
S.G.P.P., 1970, p. 45.

II

Let us pass from the obvious game of communication to that of simultaneously conscious and unconscious ideological circuits. From the surface equipment we descend to the subterranean and nutritious levels. The acquisition of ideologies is all the more great, their fascination all the more strong as the agents, and subjects of these ideologies are scarcely lucid with respect to the precise ideological character of their images, opinions and representations. In a sense, the detection of the ideologies exerts the pressure on the other. The French, for example, are particularly experts in speaking ironically on the ideologies of their neighbors, but will be very sensitive if one comes to reveal theirs to them, periodically or constantly...

But really, what is an ideology? I had myself been struck by two problems when I began to devote my time 15 years ago to researches or teaching in the history of philosophy. In order to understand the speech of the great *theocrats* (Bonald, Maistre, La Mennais, in his early works) against Rousseau, it was necessary for me to have recourse not directly to the toxt of the spiritual father of the French Revolution, but to a larger and more diffuse context to the current diffusion. I needed to learn about Rousseauism through newspapers, posters, republican tracts, etc. rather than knowing Rousseau. Even some 30 years later, in order to understand the existential revolt of young Kierkegaard, it was necessary to know a Hegelianism in fashion among the students of Copenhagen rather than the texts of Hegel themselves. And one could elongate the list of isms: neopositivism, existentialism, structuralism. All this

74

drives us to the first definition of ideology. I borrow it from Antonio Gransei: "Ideologies are the mass aspect of all philosophical conception."[6] This very suggestive definition presents, nevertheless, the inconvenience of putting more emphasis on the conscious, I would even say the strategic aspect of ideology. Now the acquisition of an ideology procedes more from unperceived mechanisms which it brings into play. Here we rediscover an idea--Aristotelian. Ah yes! Our working group, the center of Mass Communication Studies (CECMAS) exhumed the notion of *eikos* or this synonym of *endoscon* from the lucid observer of mechanisms of opinion and public discourse who was Aristotle. The *probability (vraisemblable)*, as we have translated it--and published in no. 11 of the review *Communications*[7]--is not at first close to *reality (vrai)*: this last sense of the word was recognized only in the 16th and 17th centuries. In the mind of Aristotle probability is that which *mimics the truth*, that which gives itself the *attributes of truth*. In other words, probability comes from the self, it takes as its guarantee the very evidence of things and natural evidence of the world. This naturalization of the probable opinion causes the spreading of the notion that it is certain. Probability generates the commonly received. From that time onwards it becomes the support and the resort of ideology. Probability is the form which structures the ideological contents and themes. Images, ideas and representations become ideological insofar as they submit to the form, by the natural evidence of probability.

---

[6] *Il Materialismo storico e la filosofia di Benedetto Croce*, Turin, Einaudi, 1954, p. 217.

[7] Paris, Le Seuil, 1968.

This second definition allows elucidation of a complex
problem. One heard it said that the decade 1960-1970 saw
everywhere over the world the dilution of the great ideologies. (This current opinion has regressed no doubt in regard to the recent violent awakening of utopias.) But an
ideology in its very operation is noted for the supplemen-
tary forms which structure it doubly: either the narrative,
the legendary and mythical, or the conceptual system of
reference, a system ready to caution such catechism. When
the mythical or conceptual forms blur, a residue remains
with the probable form: the ideology reduced to itself,
probability becomes current change, daily bread, common
mentality. Who is not *social* or yet *future-oriented* today,
for example? Here is an interesting example addressed to
moralists. I take it from a manual of casuistry used by
confessors of the 18th century.[8] In wintry weather, Vinebaude turned out his wife Batilde, who was guilty of being
pregnant by another before marriage, about which she had
said nothing. The whole case is conducted in such a way
as to equalize the two guilts: the cruelty of Vinebaude
and the fault of Batilde. Now the guilt of the outraged
husband is all the more great because the spouse is of *a*
social condition equal to his. In other words, in the 18th
century, responsibilities between members of the same middle
class seemed--probably--greater. In our time, probability
is reversed: responsibility increases for the poor Batilde!

A strong ideology, a *mystique* as one said in the 40's,
brought mythical narrative and simplified concepts to ideo-

---

[8]Pontas, *Dictionnaire des cas de conscience ou déci-
sion*, reedited by Migne, 1847.

logical probability. One could have put forward the idea that
myth reposes on a narrative structure and that current ideology
on a discursive structure, or quasi-discursive.

Here are several examples which illustrate how far ideological acquisition exerts pressure by the play of evidence.

First example of ideological evidence: the *Guide Bleu*,
one of the most common for French tourists. In principle, in
manifest theory, all that which is beautiful is to be seen according to a strict hierarchical model: three stars, two
stars, one star, capital and small letters, in bold type, in
italics, etc. But other hierarchies may intervene: that of
the convenience of automobile traffic, that of the cultural
antiquity. Let us see this last notion at work: "Sens, St.
Stephen's Cathedral...begun about 1130, the foundation and
main walls completed by 1160, the facade *only dates from* the
end of the 12th century; the bell-tower of St. Gavin, a 12th
century church, the bell-tower itself and its fortification
only date from the 14th century", "St. Cecile of Albe, built
from 1222 to the end of the 14th century, the tower *only dates
from* the 15th century".--"Toulouse, Asserat Hotel, built from
1555 to 1558, the gallery on the wall *only dates from* the 17th
century."[9] All of this functions according to an apparently
rigorous logic, subconscious for the most part, the logic of
probability. The tourist is in an unusual state--feeling
half guilty--where time is not money. It is important to make
profitable the time allotted for visits, to find a cultural

_____

[9] Jules Gritti and Michel Souchon, *La Sociologie face aux
Media*, Paris, Mame, 1968, pp. 121-122.

profitability. The centuries become the instrument of cultural bookkeeping. Ideology of the accountable culture.[10]

Last example in the answers of Marcelle Segal, one of our most eminent French specialists of answers to letters of the heart in the feminine press. What is the most sacred duty of man? Surely his profession. Witness the following case: a man who is director of a theatrical company says that he has a professional obligation to embrace actresses. But he complains to be in a quandary between this obligation and the jealousy of his wife. Answer of the oracle: "It is necessary to choose, it is pure Corneille" (*Elle*, 27, April 1967). As regards the woman, her inalienable sacred task will be her biological maternity: "To go out? Leave the home? A mother of four children can never leave, so to speak, and she does not want to leave because of the little ones" (*Elle*, 13, April 1967). (For the French, the term "little one" rather than that of "child" has biological, indeed animal, repercussions. Thus the social roles apportion themselves according to timeless and sacred norms: to man, profession, to woman, procreation.

Endowed with a probable form, with a speech (*enthymème*) in which the premises come from the self and implant themselves in the very nature of things, ideology develops its acquisition simultaneously in the conscious and in the subconscious, in the *mentalities*. Here we rediscover the *predogmatic* elements in which historians of doctrines, heresies, theologies, know there is more and more importance. Power

---

[10]One may find analogous considerations in Hans Magnus Enzensberger, *Culture ou mise en condition* (translated from the German), Paris, Julliard, 1965.

simultaneously more obscure and profound than that of the
strategies of communication of which we talked in the first
part. But power *of whom* and power *over whom*? Let us go back
to the example of rumor. It would be naïve to believe that
one could quelch a rumor by incarcerating the loudest rumor-
mongers--by the way, a goodly number of Christians make proof
of this naïvety when they say: it is the fault of journalists
that one talks of too many wild Eucharists or marriages of
priests.--Rumor comes from a place which is difficult to determine and circulates according to haphazard ways. The
source grows indistinct, *the power of man is being diluted.*
The original responsibilities are difficult to assign. On
the other hand, the power *over whom* grows firmer. Ideology
manifests a power which emanates from an *it* more and more
anonymous and acts on multitudes located all over the world.
Vance Packard talked of hidden persuaders.[11] One could go
on indefinitely with ideology as anonymous persuasion.

III

From *he*, the third person, we will pass to the neuter:
one or *it*, one talks, it talks. We arrive in some cultural
sub-stratum where constraining, indeed inevitably necessary
powers are exerted. We encounter codes, that is, systems of
relations which constitute languages from spoken language to

---

[11]*La persuasion Clandestine* (translated from the American),
Paris, Calman-Levy, 1958.

the cultural perception of a sensitive world. My own field
of research (the structural rhetoric of ideologists), in
quest of an operative model, made me bring together two
human sciences: narrative analysis and ethnology, both
model sciences for the detection of codes; in other words,
these sciences, which have gone beyond the empirical stage,
construct a logical *schema*; plunge them into reality in order
to separate the codes and structures. Here the word *structural* is to be taken in its strictest sense beyond the ideological snobisms and inflations. Beforehand, it would have
been necessary to take examples from linguistics and even
more precisely from phonology. Besides, I could, through
textual analyses, be a witness of the introduction of an
analogous problem into psychoanalysis.

The phonology of Nickolas Troubetzkoy and Roman Jakob-
son has shown, among other results, how the ternary code--
triangle of vowels or consonants--presides over the cutting
out of the little sonorities, to their setting apart from the
mass of available sounds, to their reciprocal configuration
of such a kind that the little sonorities become the minimal
unities, the distinctive unities of the language. A double
opposition, for example, constitutes the vowel triangle:

a

u   i

<u>a</u> *compact* stands opposite the vowels <u>u</u> and <u>i</u>, <u>u</u> *grave* stands
opposite <u>i</u> *aigu*. Homologous relationships constitute the
triangle of consonants.

k

p   f

80

Phonology unveils these strict codes in which cultural constraint is totally unconscious. Thus by the whole world and from time immemorial, twenty to thirty phonemes or little distinctive unities furnish a codified material which will compose the unities provided with meaning (words, or rather *monemes*). Emile Benveniste, in a moving homage, pays tribute to the anonymous establishment of these models which were the alphabets: "It is also necessary to render justice to these precursors who were not grammarians and whose work survives, generally anonymous, fundamental and unrecognized, so present in every moment of our lives that we no longer notice them: I mean the inventors of the modern alphabet (...). We have the oldest models of analysis in these alphabets."[12]

There is a second surprise which analyses of language will provide for us. If we pass from the alphabet to the lexicon--from phonemes to monemes--the constraining rigour of the codes diminishes somewhat, admits the influence of usage, but remains no less strong and largely unconscious. If we agree to the phrase, to the proposition, to the state-ments (segments which actually give rise to the most diffi-cult and thrilling research), the codes admit a certain liberty with stylistic variations, but a liberty restricted by rhetorical codes and writings. On the other hand, if we agree to the larger unities with narratives and myths, again the codes reassume their strict control. Thus language is greatly constrained, codified at both ends: the alphabet: narrative rules.

Our laboratory, CECMAS, may without excessive immodesty claim to have contributed to a serious elaboration of narra-

---

[12]*Problèmes de linguistique général*. Paris, Gallimard, 1966, p. 24.

tive analysis:[13] constituting of sequences, distribution of
roles or actants, ternary rhythms, mythical character of the
beginning and of the end...all is all more constraining,
codified as the narratives are popular and traditional. As
high as one ascends in human cultures one finds narrative
and in the narratives the same fundamental rules.

Thus the cutting up of sequences. All sequence is of
an alternative nature: it opens and closes by installation
and the conclusion of a binary opposition. This could be
sharp surgical opposition: the disjunction between a and b
and such a way that a or b prevailing, eliminates the other:
he will recapture/he will not recapture; he will vanquish/or
be vanquished: he will get well/he will not get well. Thus
in the face of the serious illness of John XXIII, the international press goes immediately into a state of *suspense*, installs the disjunctive code: will he get well/will he not get
well? On the third day of the Pope's illness, the popular
newspaper *France-Soir* dramatized similar contrast in pointing
out the arrival of a miraculous remedy in Rome: some "horse
plasma"! Let us say that disjunction takes on an activist
character. But a second alternative, also codified, proves
to be the most fatalistic type: it is a dilemma in the Aristotelian sense: whether it is a or b, the conclusion is the
same. John XXIII, a tragic situation: if he gets up he risks
hemorrhage, if he remains on his back, *suffocation*; in both
cases the result will be fatal.[14]

---

[13]*Communications*, 8, 1966, "L'analyse structural des
récits".

[14]Cf. J. Gritti, "Les derniers jours d'un grand homme",
in *Communications*, 6, 1964.

As for the code of the ternary rhythms of a narrative, one could schematize them as follows:

Narrative with a happy ending:
Good_____Bad_____Better

Narrative with a tragic ending:
Bad_____Good____Worse

I have not found a single press account concerning the agony of John XXIII which did not have him going through an improvement phase. A newspaper which seemed to drag its heels was roused late in the day to cry, "The Pope, better news, it is a miracle say the journalists". Thanks to a miracle the *Parisien Libéré* had just recaptured the structure and obeyed the code.

By dint of narrative analysis we join ethnology. The whole work of Claude Lévi-Strauss is that he moved from an empirical *ethnography* towards a model *ethnology*, and enlarged the latter into *structural anthropology*, thanks to the bringing to light of codes which govern the rules of kinship, topography of villages, the often refined classifications of *Savage Thought*, culinary rites, astronomy, mythical narratives, etc. Among the innumerable contributions, let us recall the culinary triangle:

Raw

Cooked   Rotten

homologous with that of vowels and consonants.[15] Also let us

---

[15]Cf. Claude Lévi-Strauss in *L'Arc*, no. 26, 1965, pp. 19–29.

recall the no less classical example of the dissections of
mythemes, or great constitutive unities, in the myth of
Oedipus.

> Kinship relations overestimated:
>> Oedipus marries his mother Iocaste
>> Antigone buries her brother Polynices

> Kinship relations underestimated:
>> Oedipus kills his father Laïos (...)
>> Oedipus kills his brother Polynices

> Negation of Autarchy (or the dependence
>> *vis-à-vis* nature):
>> Cadmus kills the dragon (...)
>> Oedipus sacrifices the Sphinx

> Affirmation of Autarchy:
>> Labdacos lame (...) Laïos lefthanded (...)
>> Oedipus, swollen foot.[16]

The multiple analyses of this kind lead Lévi-Strauss to
talk of a cultural combinatory disadvantage, to present the
emergence of a (human) culture as a regulatory emergence, like
passing from chaos to code. "One may say that the subconscious
is the individual lexicon where each one of us accumulates the
vocabulary of his personal history, but that this vocabulary
only acquires its significance, for ourselves and for others,

---

[16] *Anthropologie structural*, Paris, Plon, 1958, p. 236 ff.

insofar as the unconscious organizes it following its laws and makes it into speech."[17]

The code, according to Lévi-Strauss, makes the culture, makes the man. And man emerges from nature where he is the most profoundly unconscious! Paul Ricoeur could say--and Claude Lévi-Strauss accepts this saying--: "Kantism without transcendental subject."

The cultural unconscious, the combinatory unconscious according to Lévi-Strauss, does it have some analogy with that of psychoanalysis? If we believe what the dissident Jacques Lacan professes most profoundly, the unconscious is structured as a language: "Our doctrine is founded on the fact that the unconscious has the radical structure of language that a material functions there according to the laws which are revealed by the study of positive laws, the tongues which are or were effectively spoken.[18] This cannot be seen more clearly than in the linguistic graft on psychoanalysis. And Jacques Lacan to compare the hysterical nucleus of neurosis to a *monument*, the impenetrable memories of childhood to *archival documents*, character traits to a *semantic evolution*, personal history to a legend, the effects of distortions to *traces*.[19] In order to do an exegesis of the unconscious, Lacan resorts to a double rhetorical code: the vertical one of metaphor which operates diverse condensations, the, so to speak, horizontal one of

[17]*Ibid.*, pp. 224-225.

[18]*Ecrits*, Paris, Le Seuil, 1966, p. 594.

[19]*Ecrits*, p. 259.

metonymy which controls the movement of displacements. Metaphors and metonymies of the unconscious build the subject according to the imaginary organization of disguised maternal fixation, the symbolical organization, that is to say the adherence to the order of the Father, of the law, the society, the culture. This adherence is the most true but also the most veiled by maternal attachment and by rhetorical construction of the unconscious (by the *personality* of each individual). Also in the deepest part of the unconscious, we do not meet the individual, but rather the culture, the symbolic Code. And in order to complete his implacable psychoanalytic model, Lacan designs a second wall of inhibitions, which he names the foreclosure: the first wall, or *censure*, makes one individual part of my unconscious foreign to me, other with a small *o*; the second wall or foreclosure, makes the most hidden part of the unconscious the most foreign, other with a capital *O*; and this part is precisely the attachment to the order of the language of the culture, to the impersonal codes. Clinically, Jacques Lacan intends to research the nucleus of psychoses as far as the foreclosed terrain and the works of Francoise Dolto[20] attest to the clinical fruitfulness of certain institutions, at first sight, paradoxical, if not bizarre, of Lacan.

The latter, like a good heretic, invited a return directly to Freud. He effectively provoked it. Now the rereading, partly provoked by Lacan, attests to which point the cultural question of language is operative in the decisive experiments of Freud, no longer a speculative clinician. Thus

[20] *Le Cas Dominique*, Paris, Le Seuil, 1971; *Psychoanalyse et pediatrie*, Le Seuil, 1971.

H. Piron and A. Vergote citing the declaration of Freud:
"There where the that is existing, it is necessary for me
to become. It is a work of civilization which may be com-
pared to the draining of the Zuyderzee", comment: "Before
the child speaks one has already talked about him. In fact,
the human being is born and lives in a civilization which imposes on him the always incomplete task of taking up an active
part in it"[21] or yet: "It is by the means of the language
that each individual enters into a type of given culture, and
by this deed, into limited culture. It is the language which
gives him his name, in which he is educated, by which he
learns of the world, its goodness and values, and the rules
of kinship. Man is born and lives in a symbolic milieu, in
a world of meaning, which his language is the first to structure. Perhaps it is there that certain contents of dreams
have their root. Dreams which Freud remarks proceed neither
from adult life, nor from the childhood of the subject, but
that they reproduce fragments of an archaic heritage which,
marked with his ancestral experience, the child carries with
him in coming into the world, before all personal experience."[22]

If one adds to these attempts to reread a more cultural
Freud, the pressures of ethnology, of social psychiatry, of
socio-analysis..., or yet that of adventurous researchers
such as Reich or Marcuse, apart from classical psychoanalysis,
one must agree that this could not indefinitely ignore the
question of cultural codes. Freud, tardy and speculative,

---

[21]"Exercise de la psychanalyse chez Freud" in *La Psychanalyse science de l'homme*, Bruxelles, Dessart, 1970, p. 91.

[22]*Ibid.*, p. 59.

was no doubt not a great stranger to the Freud, active researcher and clinician.

Rigorous codes of phonological dissection or of mythical
narrative, combinatory cultural unconscious, cultural other
in the very depths of psychism, all this, *this* constitutes
the area of the greatest powers over man, the area of the
most profound quasi-necessity which human exploration has
never attained or even suspected up to the present day. But
where the *over* appears most operative, the *of* disappears:
this speaks, this codifies. We are in an *arkhé* of the limits
of the cultural and the trans-historical. Man as author of
powers seems to disappear and some, like Michel Foucault,
Jacques Lacan, following Nietzsche, decree his death. Some
ask themselves, what is the *Logos* which presides over these
codes and gives them such constraining necessitating power?

Dialectically our regressive *archaeological* approach
could have taken the opposite direction from the conquering
and *teleological* approach of the biologist. I have some
consciousness of what is disappointing for the moralist in
a drilling, which becomes undermined and suspect, which perhaps eliminates the question of power. In the end we arrive
at non-power, and maybe anti-power. The human sciences can
no more lay claim to a strategic power of manipulation than
they can question it.

At least the approach brings to light human humus as a
rule, as a capacity of Code and regulation. Then there
rises out of this minimum simultaneously residual and fundamental, an inalienable possibility: that of recognition of
the emergence of man, of the culture by Codes, by the systems
of rules and signs. Philosophers and theologians of Moralism
formerly made use of the concept of *natural* Law. I have the
impression that today this concept elicits an obstruction,

if not a bad conscience. A confrontation with the contribution
of human sciences, with particularly the regulatory, codifying
idea of *arkhé*, would permit one to regain what was envisaged
more or less happily in the concept of natural law: the
emergence of man by the Codes, from Nature.

Will one create in laboratory organisms which will have
human resemblances and pretentions? The response of human
science is that of the signs of the recognition of the human.
The fabricated organism of the 21st century will not be able
to be called *Man*, unless he is gifted with the Capacity of
Code, the translation of exchange of messages with historical
and prehistorical man and man of this century. The human
sciences today may die; they will at least have set the conditions for recognizing the man of tomorrow.

Jules Gritti

CHAPTER VI

Psychoanalysis, Manipulation and Ethics

As psychoanalysis belongs to the class of conjectural sciences, it does not need to establish itself as the ultimate reference in the name of what would be judged as morally good or bad in another scientific activity.[1]

The temptation certainly has existed at all times, which consists of wanting to establish an anthropology and a morality on science; to define this with aims which do not depend on its environment and to establish, based on so-called scientific laws, a certain number of truths in the name of which moral obligations and interdicts would be imposed.

Having said this we do not deny that scientific practice poses a certain number of ethical problems to researchers, nor that the apparently enlarging power of man over man worries others including those who believe to have for their mission the codification of the action of man.

Problems and worries are made more pressing today where man himself has become the object of science and the possi-

_____

1. For the bibliography we permit ourselves to refer to our work, *Le Temps de la Mort*, Cerdic-Publications, Strasbourg, 1975.

bilities of action on his being and his behavior are multiplying.

It is good to recall, however, that scientific activity has at all times made a problem for the theologian, moral or not.

Was it not Luther who saw in Copernicus "the madman who claims to overthrow all astronomy"? Did not the Scriptures declare that it is to the sun and not to the earth that Joshua had given the order to stop?

Have not the scientists who had theological preoccupations paid tribute in their stormy relations with theologians? Whether it is for Galileo in Italy and for Michel Servetus in Geneva, ecclesiastical power cannot stand the advent of a new knowledge come to perturb the quiet possession of that which one believed to be definitive.

Coming nearer to us, did not Bishop Wilberforce attack Charles Darwin's theory as immoral because it holds that man descends from the ape?

If certain scientific activities raise questions today it is not according to us because they would come, as they did in the past, to weaken a certain number of dogmatic, abstract affirmations or consider theoretical moral values. Who still worries about man's descent from the ape?

The discoveries of the laws of nature certainly put in question a global and substantial universe which had given foundation to the elaboration of moral norms and values such as the theologian deduced from the scientific theological systems of yesteryear. These discoveries gave staggering blows to the totalizing systems, indeed totalitarian. They caused the a priori scientists who had the proud complacency of censors to vacillate.

However the essential was not questioned and moral elaboration, after reestablishment, could continue to be conceived as the adaptation of human behavior to a "natural given", perceived in its intangible and irremovable reality.

With the appearance of human biology and the so-called sciences of man, the question is renewed. In fact, not only is new knowledge acquired but progress parallel to technology henceforth permits the application of this knowledge and action on their subject.

If the progress of knowledge could give a promethean dizziness to the followers of scientism, the actual possibility of applying to man and his milieu the efficacity of new techniques causes the appearance of anguished reactions which take their origin, according to us, from the impression of resentment for an always greater intrusion into which man considered until now the place of his liberty and autonomy.

One may question the reinstitution of astronomy and the pseudo-humiliation which results from the theories of Charles Darwin. On the other hand, the mastery of the mechanisms of fertilization and reproduction which one believed until now to be reserved for the determinisms of nature, a good mother who was seemingly infallible, is difficult to support. The possibility of the other, whatever it is, thanks to a knowledge of psychological mechanisms, to foresee, then to determine an activity in which one believed oneself the free subject, is properly intolerable.

One gets used to the idea of atomic revolution more easily, however terrifying it is than to the feeling of being manipulated oneself without even knowing it. The accumulation of fantastic destructive methods by nations is less agonizing than the idea that an anonymous power could place the worm in one's inner self, namely, the development of reproductive cells and free, conscious activity.

The signifers "manipulation" or "power of man over man" are connoted from phantasms of rape. One certainly admires the attainments of genetics, the power of action of the mass media which uses "psychological techniques"; but one fears to see them escape control and to become in the hands of another-- who is necessarily an enemy--an effective instrument for constructing *"the best of all worlds"* and for enslaving under its yoke the one who is deprived of this power.

The question of the limits of this power or of its useful employment, one asks oneself with all the more acuteness as one knows oneself to be the immediate possible victim. The conflict which rises from that time onwards is to be considered less of a sad reexamination of an out-of-date wisdom as a grasp of the image which man has of himself. We know how this clasp touches the most pregnant desire of all: the love which man admits for his own image, love which one technically calls narcissism.

Finally, let us note that with the recently born human sciences, one discovers not only the power of action of man over himself, but one feels again the vacillation of that which had been considered relevant in the domain of the natural or the direct action of the divine. Moral conscience itself that must govern justly the progress of science and technology, does it not result in cultural determinisms susceptible also to being manipulated by science and technology?

So then, one feels alone, terribly alone. The first cause reported to be increasingly far away, man is well obliged henceforth to accept himself as being his own providence and the question of ethics becomes urgent.

But there is also a new questioning arising operated by psychoanalysis on the subject of morality and on its basis.

At first, we have supposed that psychoanalysis as science does not have to give the ultimate reference to the name of which one might judge as a morally permissable scientific activity. Furthermore, psychoanalysis poses the question of this reference: it introduces the idea of desire in ethical elaboration and practices it in the field of civilization. Let us explain ourselves.

The object of psychoanalysis is the man, or rather the subject in linguistic relation. Fundamentally, psychoanalysis has only allowed man to speak within his culture. It takes him from the very depth of his history, transmitted and lived, and it takes him into the bosom of language within which he is bound and at the same time divided, and sets him as it were on the way by which he can make his desire understood.

The central axis of the problematic of psychoanalysis is that of body language or more precisely of the body engaged in the position of signifier. This axis upsets "classical" epistemology on which ethical elaboration is still founded. This epistemology starts from a subject which apprehends an object and knows reality. Psychoanalysis itself finishes by defining a symbolical universe where a subject, divided because he speaks, is ceaselessly in search of an object always already lost. What can one say? For the problem of being and language, we must start from a little further away.

I. EXISTENCE AND REALITY

The centuries which directly precede us bequeath the problem of the relationships of thought and language. This problem is posed with a particular acuteness in the classical age when the art of good thought was united with the art of good speech. Therefore normative art, with which experts try with a scrupulous modesty to establish rules by dint of great catalogs and rigourous explanations, for the better advantage of social, indeed intellectual morality.

Moving from a problem of the relationships of thought with nature (and with the supernatural) after the Renaissance, because of a greater insistence on the workings of the mind and on this faculty uniquely human, namely, reason, one asks the question about the relationships of thought to language, the operations of the former determining the organization of the latter.

With the 17th century and the project of "General Grammar", what changes is the accent placed on language rather than on the reality, and from there on the particular importance of the verb "to be".

With Arnauld, Lancelot and Nicole, "The function of language is the *representation* of thought",[2] and further still, it is the representation of logical thought. It is therefore no longer so much the *reality* of instituted relationships but

---

2. O. Ducrot and T. Todorov, *Dictionnaire Encylopédique des sciences du langage*, Paris, Seuil, 1972, p. 15.

the judgment which matters, namely, the *representative power* of the words in the statement.

This representative power is located entirely in the verb "to be"; without it there is no more "substantive" than "predicate". If you will, it is the canvas background on which appear the words, nouns or adjectives.

Thus, the verb "to be" has a very particular place: it is simultaneously a word belonging to the language, and it is even the act of judgment which affirms it. "So that the verb *to be* would have essentially the function of connecting all language to representation which it designates. Being which it indicates is neither more nor less than the existence of the thought."[3]

The consequence of this elaboration is very important; it is that existence is founded in thought. This leads us besides to yet another formula, elaborated elsewhere which is that of the Cartesian *cogito*.

The transparence of the representation however soon will be obscure and will be questioned from different sides; the function of the verb has reached such an extent of generality that it will only remain for it to dissociate itself. When the proposition will not be more than the unity of syntax, one will analyse the verb as one grammmatical word among others. Whereas the power of manifestation of language still continues to be fascinating, one will question the relationships between existence and language.

------

3. M. Foucault, *Les mots et les choses, une archéologie des sciences humaines*, Paris, Gallimard, 1966, p. 110.

In what manner? Following M. Safouan, and analytical
experiment, we will say at first that:

"In order to exercise its effects on the organism, a real
object has, after all, no need to be symbolized nor need of
that which the subject has the least knowledge. In other
words, the fact that it is real, is not sufficient criterion
of its existence."[4] We add that this *real* is therefore, according to the word of Lacan, *impossible*.

-----But where does existence unfold? One realizes that in
all judgment, whatever kind it is, there is a subject which
it affirms. It is necessary for us, however, to preserve the
complete formula, that is to say, neither to isolate the subject nor the affirmation. Then we will say, "There is only
existence and the feeling of existence for a subject which
speaks." "The word does not presuppose the real, only the
language."[5]

As judgment has been traditionally defined as a speech
susceptible to being true or false, we are led to emphasize
that it is not in an intention to conform to the real (the
real always being secondary) that truth lies, but in the word.

From there we are brought back to the anteriority of
language--which only exists as *spoken*--to the structure of
the subject as subject desiring by adherence to the symbolical
order.

---

4. M. Safouan, "De la structure en psychanalyse" in
Qu'est-ce que le structuralisme? Ouvrage collectif, Paris,
Seuil, 1968, p. 260.

5. *Ibid.*

This symbolic order preexists as a third order, which only supports itself by fastening to itself the real (which makes the hole in the system) and the imaginary, which designates not the illusion but the dual relationship. It was already there and always there.

On the other hand, the word, let us say the signifier or even the signifying chain "condensed from a binarity at its interval point"[6] is simultaneously presence and absence of the thing. In the order of things, to make use of words, or signifiers, is to take one's distance with regard to those things. It is to render them present all the while maintaining their absence the very fact of the nomination.

That which is of value for the order of things may be transposed to that which one may call, for want of something better, the order of "states". The child who does not speak lives of "himself" without any mediation as satisfaction or empty. One may even conceive him as "drowned" in the mute perception of a joy or distress mythically expressed as absolute.

With the cry comes the first difference.[7] If the cry detracts a first time from the urgency of the event, if it opens

---

6. J. Lacan, *Écrits*, Paris, Seuil, p. 843.

7. "It is a fact of extreme importance to see that this association of a sound (equally giving rise to motor images of the subject himself) with a perception which is already itself a complex, may increase the 'hostile' character of the object and serve to direct attention toward a perception. Our own cries confer character to the object, while otherwise, and because of the suffering, we could not have any qualitatively clear idea." S. Freud, *La naissance de la psychanalyse*, p. 377.

a crack in the rule of things and states, it will be necessary that the words come following--phonemes--in order to arrange, in repeating the crack, the sides of the fault thus open.

In order to be brief, let us say that the cry inaugurates the rupture of the inaugural continuity before the existence of need receives from the Other phonemes and monemes in order to "appropriate the signifier under which it succumbs".[8]

The infant has access to the symbolic relationship when he may signify himself from "an *elsewhere* to the place where he is situated and with which he coincides"[9] and this *elsewhere*, which is given to him, and which will allow him to speak, necessitates the detour to an *Other* place.

But what is this Other?

"The Other is...the *place* (we emphasize) where the I is formed, who speaks with the one who listens, what the one says being already the response and the other deciding to listen whether one has spoken or not."[10] The Other is this third auditor always assumed, necessary for any act of word, word to which he gives rise. Thus, one may say that the Other is the place of language insofar as the latter exists with respect to the subject in an alterity "as radical as that of still undecipherable hieroglyphics in the solitude of the desert".[11] But the Other, for Lacan, is also the "witness

---

8. Lacan, *Écrits*, p. 843.

9. A. de Waelhens, "La paternité et le complexe d'Oedipe" in *L'Analyse du langage théologique*, Paris, Aubier-Montagne, 1969, pp. 247-256.

10. Lacan, *Écrits*, p. 431.

11. *Ibid.*, p. 550.

to the Truth", insofar as being the place of the word: "Thus it is from elsewhere than from the Reality which it concerns that the Truth takes its guarantee: it is from the Word."[12]

This means that it is in the relationship of the word and to the word that the small man has access to his "being" as a subject (which will reveal itself soon as that of one lacking of being) and to his "humanity".

Because he of necessity passes through the mother or her substitute, who occupies the place of the Other, to realise the specific action which fulfills his needs, which he himself is incapable of achieving because of his *Hilflosigkeit*,[13] it is by the question that the child will have access to the symbolic order and to the order of signifiers, signifiers that he will soon take to his own account to express his wants and his world.

But these signifiers are the signifiers of the Other and "to enter into the language, to undertake to exist and to define oneself for others through the word, the subject loses himself, effaces himself necessarily as the subject of his own enunciation".[14] We will come back to this.

The assumption by the infant of the Code of the Other means that there is something he cannot explain of himself.

---

12. *Ibid.*, p. 808.

13. Here one sees the converging of need (of care and food), and the significant relationship to the Other, the place of language occupied by the mother, the converging which will reveal itself soon, and we will see it farther along as an impasse.

14. C. Conte and M. Safouan, "Sexualité" in *Encyclopaedia universalis*, 14, (Paris, 1972), p. 925.

That part of him which is lost because it cannot be expressed
constitutes for Freud the sense of the primary or original
feeling of liberation which divides and simultaneously constitutes the subject as a subject of desire. This original feeling of liberation is postulated by him as founder of the unconscious. It is the first "setting aside" of the conscious,
the first loss and the most radical around which the other
representations of impulse will congregate later.

The division between the conscious and the unconscious,
between that which is spoken and the one who speaks, between
the subject of the statement and the subject of the stating,
operates from the moment of the entrance of the subject into
language. Language is the condition of the unconscious, and
the division of the subject is an effect of the language.
Let us examine this more closely.

II. THE SUTURE

What place does this subject occupy with respect to language, with respect to the chain of signifiers? This is what
we may develop at present.

For this, let us return to the question of judgment. This
is, as we have said, defined traditionally as a speech susceptible to being true or false. If, on the other hand, the truth
is not found in an intention to conform to the real but in the
word, a question is raised. In fact, if judgment consists of
affirming a relationship between two words and that this relationship is one of identity, what is it, in the word, which
permits to present this identity as such? It is a question

of the problem of the very nomination and as it is the subject which nominates, what will happen to this subject?

For the essential, we refer the reader to the article of J. A. Miller, entitled "La Suture".[15] The author starts from the reflexion of G. Frege on arithmetic.[16]

G. Frege questions the progression of whole natural numbers and its basis. What is the initial position of "the distinctive unity"? Miller shows that this unity, the *one*, does not maintain itself otherwise than being already identical to itself, which is true also for any number from one on. Thus the definition of identity presupposes that the unity is identical to itself and if *one* cannot be substituted for *one*, the "truth" is subverted.

However, there must be somewhere a unity which is not identical to itself, without which the system remains at a standstill. If one supposes, for example, that *one* is identical to *one*, and that furthermore one substracts *one* from *one*, what remains? The spontaneous response is *zero*, and not *one*. What then is the function of this *zero* which suddenly appears?

Zero is the postulation of a number which would not be identical to itself. It simply marks the border, the limit of the system, the unheard emergence into reality of a thing not identical to itself. There is not any doubt about this, *zero* figures in the continuation of numbers as being itself a number and if one puts the number two and one asks how many

---

15. J. A. Miller, "La Suture" in *Cahiers pour l'analyse*, No. 1, Paris, Seuil, 1966 [1970], pp. 39-51.

16. G. Frege, *Die grundlagen der arithmetik*, Breslau, W. Koebner, 1884.

numbers preceed two, one responds two, in fact there is one
and zero. The number zero is counted for one when its concept answers to "nothing", to a thing which will not be identical to itself.

Therefore in this paradox there is a lacuna in the continuity of numbers, which one introduces in the chain symbol-
izing it by *one*, and immediately it is excluded by losing its
meaning, although it remains present in power. The paradox
consists in the fact that no (arithmetical) operation is possible if this impossible object is not *simultaneously* summoned
and rejected, admitted *and* excluded.[17]

Miller affirms that the "weakest point of resistance" of
logical discourse, that which assures at the same time its
closing or its suture is the *zero* taken insofar as the number
assigned to the concept of non-identity to self. And the
author of recognition in the relationship of *zero* to the continuation of numbers, the most elementary articulation of the
relationship which the subject maintains with the chain of
signifiers. The subject is this "impossible object" which
the discourse summons and rejects, *wanting to know nothing
about it.*

---

17. The repetition in the series of numbers is maintained
by the fact that whatever zero lacks passes, according to a
primarily vertical axis, removing the barrier which limits the
field of verticality in order to represent itself as one, suppressing next its own meaning in each of the names of the numbers in the metonymical chain of successional progression.
Miller, "La Suture", *loc. cit.*, p. 48.

The text concludes, "Its exclusion (of the subject) outside of the discourse which internally he intimates: suture."[18]
That this suture has been constantly felt, to be challenged
is precisely that which defines the position of psychoanalysis,
and with regard to speech, ethical or not (including his own).
The structure of the subject as "the fluttering in eclipses"
(Miller), makes the subject excluded, returned to the very
fact that he speaks, there is that which still asks to be in-
terrogated. We find the field of this interrogation in linguistics.

III. SIGN AND SIGNIFIER

"Language, without which nothing is designated, is func-
tionally antipathetic to the designation of that which designates as such, that is to say, that which we will call the
pure subject, or more simply, the subject which speaks."[19]
Thus a problem is brought to light which is known to linguistics, at the present time that is the distance which separates
the two processes of an act of speech: the process of enunciation and the announcement itself. In all speech, the subject
indicated in the statement (the "shifter") is distinguished
from that which produces the enunciation itself. If there is

18. Miller, "La Suture", *loc. cit.*, p. 149.

19. Safouan, *De la structure en psychanalyse*, p. 252.

no longer this separation and the two subjects blend together,
one will have only an imperceptible murmur, the statement will
be ultimate and total, it will have succeeded in including
also the one who speaks.

Psychoanalysis pushes this distance until it makes a
barrier. In fact if the talking subject cannot be signified
nor designated absolutely by its word, we must not see there
an effect of human insufficiency, but an effect of the language
which *divides* the subject. In other words, the subject does
not know what he does when he talks. "There is a desire because there is the unconscious, that is to say language which
escapes from the subject in structure and effect, and because
there is always at the level of language something which is beyond the conscious and it is there that may be situated the
function of desire."[20]

In order to make precise the relationship of the subject
to the signifier, it is necessary to start from what Lacan
calls the "unifying trait". This unifying trait is the primary identification (to the first signifier), which operates
in the first demand apart from maternal power. "Only take a
signifier as a sign of this total power, that is to say of
this total power in all its strength, and of this birth of
possibility, and you have the unifying trait which, to fill
the invisible mark which the subject takes from the signifier,
alienates the subject in the first identification which forms
the ideal of the me."[21]

20. J. Lacan, "Psychanalyse et Médicine" in *Lettres de
l'Ecole Freudienne*, No. 1, p. 45.

21. Lacan, *Ecrits*, p. 808.

The unary trait is the trait of the one, the trait of the identical. The subject identifies itself with this trait, but in identifying itself with the identical, it is alienated, the subject being fundamentally heterogenous to the signifier. If the signifier represents the subject, it is as a non-identical. We have seen with J. A. Miller, the importance of these remarks in that which concerns the relationship of the subject to the signifying chain. If then the signifier represents the subject (and represents it as the non-identical), it follows that the relationship of the signifier to the signified is broken, distorted, that is to say, that there is no longer correspondence between the signifier and the signified.

Thus the very idea of the sign worked out by F. de Saussure is requestioned by psychoanalysis. The definition of a sign proposed by this Genevese scholar may be summarily stated in the following fashion: the sign is the union of an acoustical image (for the oral sign) called *signifier* and a concept called *signified*. This sign, which is entirely in the domain of language (as much from the signifier aspect as the signified aspect) is also in a bond with a *referent* in reality.[22]

Saussure accompanies the description of the linguistic sign with explicatory diagrams. From among many others, let us reproduce this one:[23]

---

22. F. De Saussure, *Cours de linguistique générale*, Paris, Payot, 1916 [1969], p. 98f.

23. *Ibid.*, p. 158.

In *L'instance de la lettre dans l'inconscient*, Lacan takes up again what he calls Saussurian "algorithme", but presents it in this form:[24]

$$\frac{S}{s} \quad \text{which equals} \quad \frac{\text{signifier}}{\text{signified}}$$

One may make several remarks on the subject of the difference between these two formalizations:

---Saussure's diagram is reversed by Lacan: the signifier is above the line, the signified underneath.[25] Moreover, the parallelism in which signifier and signified were placed is broken, even in the typography: capital S and small s (written in italics).

---The double reversed arrows which frame the diagram of Saussure's sign, which indicate the indissociability of the sign in both aspects, have disappeared. But this symbol has its importance: it indicates that to all change of the signifier there must be a corresponding change in the signified, just as all modification in the signified must bring one about in the interior of the signifier. This means that for linguistics, the construction of the signifier and of the signified is subordinate to the previous pattern of the sign; the signifier is an amorphous mass which is organized by joining itself to a concept which comes out of another mass equally amorphous without this union.

---

24. *Ibid.*, p. 497.

25. That which was said to J. L. Nancy and P. Lacoue-Labarthe in their commentary on *L'Instance,* (*Le titre de la lettre* coll. à *la lettre*, Paris, Ed. Galilée, 1973, p. 55), in which Lacan puts the sign back on its feet.

---To suppress the arrows is correlative to another suppression: that of the ellipse which encloses the sign (and symbolizes its structural unity) of Saussure. This operation succeeds in fact in striking out the sign itself. In suppressing the ellipse, Lacan requestions the relationship of representation of reality by the sign.

One may note the consequences on three levels. First, the question of the referent (or of reference in reality) arises--and it rises before all because the referent determined the position of the signified, of the concept.

The signified afterwards as it is separated from the referent, begins to "float". One may say in another way that the concept becomes "undecidable". Let us cite Lacan: "The idea of an incessant sliding of the signified under the signifier therefore compels recognition.[26] One guesses already that the signification is only maintained through recourse to the only signifier.

The last consequence, we will note in a double way. First it is evident that the line which F. de Saussure traces between the signified and the signifier has thickened: it has become (moreover that is how Lacan began his commentary on "L'algorithme") *a barrier resistant to signification*.[27] The reinforcement of the line is correlative to the suppression of the ellipse. It leads finally to that which one may call the autonomisation of the signifier, insofar as it is no longer one of the aspects of the sign, but that it holds its own in some way.

---

26. *Ibid.*, p. 502.

27. *Ibid.*, p. 497 (emphasis is ours).

To sum up, we may recall what this operation which Lacan practices on the sign manifests.

One realizes on one hand that it is not a question of desire in linguistics, only more than it is a question of the subject.[28]

On the other hand, it seems that reality is imposed "naturally" on its designation, on its representation by language. The raising of this last idea, which is above all a heritage of classical thought, we have seen in part, leads to the question of language, of language as much as for us is spoken, that is to say, that it supposes subjects, and it implies a demand, a desire. Afterwards this questioning demands the materialization of language (or of the signifier) and the differential structure.

In other words, there is only spoken language, it is necessary for us to announce the anteriority of the subject over the signifier. But this relationship is circular in fact (without being reciprocal), because if the signifier *represents the subject*, the latter is also the *effect of the*

---

28. Modern linguistics (synchronic) is in fact constituted as scientific in operating the distinction between language and word: "In separating language and word, one separates at the same time: first that which is social from that which is individual; second that which is essential from that which is accessory and more or less accidental." F. de Saussure, *Cours de linguistique générale*, p. 30. The effect of linguistics on the language reveals, as non-scientific, the field of the word. It is with the word (and the hearing) precisely that psychoanalysis begins. Let us note here directly that according to us, it is necessary to retranspose this language-word distinction in the field of ethics in order to discern the origin of the conflict.

signifier, that is to say, *that it only appears as such after the introduction of the signifier.*

This linguistic detour is not useless for our purpose. It permits us to specify the relationships of the subject which is represented in the signifying chain although the latter remains at the same time in a radical alternation with respect to it.

IV. ENJOYMENT AND SIGNIFICATION

Before making any specific points about the power of man over man and its limits, it is still necessary for us to specify the idea of the object as psychoanalysis conceives it, that of the subject having been evoked. This precision will permit us hence to indicate enjoyment.

We have already mentioned that it is by demand that the child has access to the symbolic order. This demand bears on the satisfaction of his needs.

Demand is of language and language as such addresses itself to the Other from which it has come. Demand conceived as such, demand in itself addressing the Other asks for "something other than the satisfaction (of needs). It is the demand for a presence or an absence".[29] It is addressed to the Other, it is a word to itself before it becomes a question about the lack which is felt from the fact of language. It

---

29. Lacan, *Ecrits*, p. 690-691.

110

is thus that the satisfaction of needs only deprives the
child of the only way by which the needs are satisfied and
that the privilege attributed to the Other is established,
the privilege to give what he has not. "This is," says Lacan,
"what is called his love."[30]

Love, defined thusly, as the gift of that which one has
not, as the relationship of one subject in need to another
subject in need, returns in a decisive way to the fundamental
expropriation which is operated by the entry into language.

This expropriation of the being of the subject will join
to that which of necessity is alienated (since this can only
be indicated and therefore satisfied by demand). Also by going by the way of the signifier, the need in its turn, and the
object of the need becomes the signifier in/of the relationship. Desire thus "is outlined in the margin where demand
tears itself away from need".[31]

The object of need is, in the demand, transmuted "into
proof of love"[32] and that which loses itself from it to being
elevated to the function of signifier, reappears from the
other side of the demand; it will function as the object of
desire, which henceforth will envisage objects, according to
the line of language, across the mechanisms of the substitution and the combination (of condensation and deplacement)
that language prescribes. The object may be substituted insofar as one has to make the order of substitution possible,

---

30. *Ibid.*, p. 691.

31. *Ibid.*, p. 814.

32. *Ibid.*, p. 691.

therefore to the order of the signifier or of "the connection of signifier to signifier which permits elision, by which the signifier installs the lack of the being in the relationship of the object, by making use of the value of return of the signification in order to invest it with the desire having in view this lack which it supports".[33] If, facing the divided subject, the real, as one has seen it, does not determine the position of the signified, since there is no existence apart from language, we can interrogate ourselves, even if this interrogation is confined to myth, on that which may well be the "referent" of language.

With the first demand, the need is *alienated*: the mother, which is the place of the Other, satisfies the need. There is in a *"first satisfaction"*[34] "intolerable", inexpressible enjoyment and this satisfaction blazes a trail, an opening, a place where pleasure may be renewed. But, let us emphasize, the child believes that it is the pleasure and the desire of the mother, so that it is around her, her presence-absence, that the dialectic of demand and desire comes together.

With the demand, we have said, the needs will be filtered by the ways of the structure of the signifier. What is lost of the subject (is repressed) will follow the "beaten paths", and will model itself according to the metaphorometonymic laws of the primary process.

---

33. *Ibid.*, p. 515.

34. See for further details, Freud, *Esquisse d'une psychologie scientifique* in *La Naissance...*, p. 336.

The primary processes envisage, says Freud,[35] "an identity of perception". This can only be lacking: in fact the system which perceives cannot be the same as that which has recorded the trace of the first satisfaction, if not how would a new perception be possible? Also, if the first experience can only be rediscovered as trace, this trace will necessarily be different from the perception since it is henceforth integrated to a trace system[36] which one may identify among the signifiers.

The identity of perception can only be therefore always *lacking* given that the satisfaction, to which it should turn back, is definitely lost, that it can no longer be re-presented, that is to say, simultaneous presence and exclusion of this presence.

Then, failing the fusion with the mother, forbidden also because named, failing the Sovereign Good, the possibility presents itself anyway to direct the desire toward another object. Thus with desire, that which establishes itself in the word as the reference, is enjoyment, forbidden enjoyment.

The mother turns the question of his desire for her to a third party: beyond the real father, to Name of the Father, making the latter a signifier at first, a signifying law. Thus no response is given, and yet the gift of the signifier constitutes the obstacle, the limit. With it and it only, enjoyment is forbidden. The speech then will only be able to signify the enjoyment by going beyond the law which forbids

---

35. *Ibid.*, p. 342ff.

36. C. Conte and M. Safouan, "Sexualité humaine" in *Encyclopaedia Universalis*, 14 (Paris, 1972), p. 925.

that it should be stated in its entirety. "To talk of enjoyment, is to implant barriers which were removed for the benefit of my pleasure, and which mutilated my speech so that, as
happens with truth, it can only be half expressed."[37] The enjoyment is therefore an *absent signifier*, it may not be represented otherwise than by substitutes for this absent signifier.

Ordering of language rests on a hole, a lack. In the
dialectic of demand and desire, at the moment of the Oedipus,
another dialectic, that of being and having, centers itself
around the phallus. The child, who wants existence, is brought
back to the father who possesses it. The phallus is precisely
that which one neither is nor has. Resistant to the dialectic
of the demand, it must pass by a negativation in order to become, as a symbolic phallus, the key of desire. It renders
them present in language what cannot be figured: sex, the
difference.

One cannot have the phallus: it will therefore be the
sign of the impossible object. One cannot be it, the phallic
symbol will occupy this point where the Other itself is lacking, missing. The phallus will be the signifier of enjoyment.
Thus the phallus places itself with the Other, as "the very
signifier of the impossibility of the signifier to engender
a univocal signified";[38] in other words it is in a metaphorical position and its dehiscence in fact goes back to nothing
other than the plan of repression itself.

---

37. J. D. Nasio, "Métaphore et phallus" in S. Leclaire,
Démasquer le réel. Un essai sur l'objet en psychanalyse,
Paris, Seuil, 1971, p. 107.

38. C. Conte and M. Safouan, "Phallus" in *Encyclopaedia
Universalis,* 12 (Paris, 1972), p. 915.

Consequently, one may say, following Nasio, that the metaphorical signifier produces (1) an effect of signification which one may note also as an effect of truth; (2) an effect of the signified (on which the rhetoricians have insisted).

---An effect of signification. The child can only have access to the status of the desiring subject if he breaks his imaginary identification with the phallus, and if he is marked by castration. The phallus, which is understood as the very cause of desire, may then represent the subject (and represent it for another signifier). *The subject may speak.* He is present at each moment of accomplishment of the signifying chain counting as "one more" at the same time, that he is at each time counted out, eliminated. But what is said about him, what is manifest of his desire, is never the "proper sense". In the absurdity of dreams, in the incongruity of mistakes, there is no truth which should be extracted; there is simply the possibility of speaking all over again, to interpret, if one wishes, in order to construct a new text. The truth is in these deformed traces. We have said that it is in the word, which means that it is precisely in the eccentricity of the subject and the desire, in this fact that the subject of the statement never agrees with that which is stated. To interpret is therefore to always feel the suture, but without ever having finished with it.

---An effect of the signified. We just saw that signification is always in company, because the subject and the desire which are indicated in the word *will never be* completely what they say. For that reason one believes that in the effect of the sense of the metaphor there is an "effect of the signified". Rhetoricians certainly know that the word making a metaphor does not have its usual expected meaning. They see the emergence of

a new signifier, which is substituted for the other. If
there is a metaphor in a text, that is to say, an incongruity
between signifiers, one will try to lessen the divergence
with a view to amplification and new signifiers: one will
make an image out of them.

"To construct a metaphor, to take it as an image, it is
a repetition of the formation of the Me insofar as the Me has
its origin in the passions for the altered image of the body."
"This Me," adds Nasio, and we will come back to this, "is in
truth only reversed lines of its own image, it is an object,
it is nothing";[39] and the author cites Lacan: "This subject
who thinks he can have access to himself, can designate himself in the statement is nothing other than such an object."

Indeed, this Me object of love of which clinical science
describes the advent with the mirror phase,[40] is presented as
a new object in the quest for the lost object. The Me, image
of the self returned by the mirror or the like, substitute
for the desire which is given as the desiring subject, this
Me place of lure, if it is so, is engulfed in the place left
empty and will henceforth mediate the relationship to the
other....It is Me that I see when I look at you, it is Me

39. Nasio, "Métaphore et phallus", *loc. cit.*, p. 112.
The quotation which Nasio introduces here in the text is
given from Lacan (*Ecrits*, p. 828). We allow ourselves to
refer expressly to this page, insofar as the metaphor opens
to it, between two texts, horizons well suited to striking
one's understanding.

40. We refer the reader to the article of J. Lacan, "Le
stade du miroir comme formateur de la fonction du Je telle
qu'elle nous est révélée dans l'expérience psychanalytique"
in *Ecrits*, pp. 93-100.

that I love when I love you: I love myself loved by you or I
love you loving me....

This image, this *form* of the assumed Me and which one
says and believes is really and truly oneself, is only a Me.
If it is loved it is because the mother declared it loveable,
it is because the proof of the test by the other gave to him
honorable mention, that he believes himself thus worthy of
displaying his existence.

To take then, the effect of the sense of the metaphor as
an image and this image as an object, is to fill in what has
appeared as a hole, as a gap. To enjoy the effect of the
signified, is to find oneself in the reflections in the mirror
which bring to life the form of the body, in a metaphorical
word which becomes "erotisized word". It is indeed to establish the logical order of the image and of wisdom...and this
order is significant.

The body, the object, however are not "of language". The
object is also off center with respect to what the statement
designates as the object of need or of demand. And this object is also always lacking, always *lost*, since the subject
is never finished with the work of signification, with desire.
It is still necessary that the object constitutes itself an
object lacking. It must leave the hole of a marked absence.
It is that which designates the phallus, in as much as it is
a sign of castration, that is to say, "sign itself of the
latency which is the mark of everything signifiable, consequently that it is elevated (...) to the function of a signifier".[41] The vanishing point which denotes the lack of the

---

41. Lacan, *Ecrits*, p. 692.

object is constituted by a sign, the result of ceasing of signification: a signifier is fixed, ceases to represent the subject and becomes the sign which refers to the object at the time when the latter is something else.[42] "The sign of the object, it is that which represents something else for someone and the signifier component of this sign is each metonymic feature which will impress in an infinite concatenation the movement of desire."[43]

The signified component of this sign may become a known, as we have just seen. The signified taken in an image is knowledge which one may enjoy (but how, if not by perversion?). One does realize that knowledge is not truth, that it is just as separate from the truth as it is from enjoyment. Knowledge wishes to be always wholistic, it would like to know the ultimate on life and death. In this respect it is equally the forbidden object. This allows one to comprehend that one may enjoy it in transgression.

You will not attain equality for the signifier, you will not fill the lack of the Other; you will not know, you will remain divided, you will not have the complete power....At each time, with castration it is death which introduces itself into existence. And it is death which makes life.

---

42. The signifier, "is that which represents a subject for another signifier" (Lacan, *Ecrits*, p. 819); "the sign, is that which represents something for someone" (*ibid.*, p. 840).

43. Nasio, in S. Leclaire, *Démasquer le réel*, p. 110.

V. SOME CONSEQUENCES

What is there of "manipulation" and "power of man over man" in all that? All and nothing; indeed, psychoanalysis insists on the anteriority of language and structure, which determine the accession to subjectivity. Psychoanalysis maintains that there is only spoken language, that the signifying chain functions because of a missing signifier, because of an emptiness: "The reduction of the subject to its cause, without being its own cause, *can only be accomplished under the necessary condition of an imperfect system of signifiers where there is one signifier missing.*"[44] Enjoyment is this missing signifier.

This means primarily that all which could be conceived as "innate", and "natural" tends toward the "acquired" or the "cultural"; in this sense the alienation is total and the infant is the "fruit" of all his conditioning, "manipulations", desires and his antecedents. Nothing which has been acquired, nothing which has been transmitted, nothing which has been marked in this flesh will not have access in its turn to the word. There is not a particle of skin, there is no organ which does not pass through signifiers in order to become "human".

In this sense, all is manipulation and the power of man over his fellow man and his descendants seems almost absolute. Is it not this implicit knowledge which has guided the educators of Monsieur, the brother of Louis XIV, husband of Madame

---

44. *Ibid.*, pp. 104-105.

and of the Princess Palatine, and friend of the knight of Lorraine?

This power gives rise to concern. Certain begetters... and certain benevolent jurists prefer, however, to transfer the origin of unexpected behaviour to some hormone or chromosome, which is often not the case.

What is true for the offspring of men in the 20th Century, will still be true for those which the 22nd Century will spawn in test-tubes. It will be very necessary to talk to these babies if one desires that they have access to a human form of behaviour. One will also be able to condition them as male or female, worker or warrior, according to the good will of an eventual "Big Brother".

The difference with that which we actually know, is that one might produce industrially on the assembly line the originality which today is still to be found only in craftsmen. Let us add to these futuristic views that the man of tomorrow will know better the extent of the power which he already possesses, and which is considerable, but which he still uses as Mr. Jourdain used prose.

However, tomorrow, as today, the same question will be asked: there is no subjectivity save through the signifier and the signifier represents a subject. Thus from two things come one. Or else one will allow beings born from test tubes to appeal as a subject: one will "adopt" them, or else one will produce heaps of cells which will have nothing human about them save their form. We will return later to this question of the form.

Let us say that all is apparently conditioned. The cause is to be located in the language, but because the subsistence of the signifier is of connotation (Lacan, p. 658), alienation remains incomplete. Because the signified slips ceaselessly under the signifier, the subject retains in its limited reality a limited freedom: "It is the effect of a word full of reordering past contingencies by giving them the sense of necessities to come, as they are constituted by the limited liberty by which the subject makes them present...."[45] The reordering of past contingencies is possible because the subject is divided, because it cannot attain while living equality with the signifier, because it cannot intermingle with the signifying chain. As the signified is always deferred the subject has never finished with its work of signification, with desire, and with creation. If it depends on the desire of its begetters, let us not forget that they are submitted to the same division as it is, and do not know what they desire, because they are ignorant of whence their desire comes. There remains therefore, a narrow margin, where the subject may risk what one may call its faith.

There remain "conditioning" by mass media, "alienation" by publicity, "uniformization" by directed information. It is not our intention to deny the importance of this, rather to emphasize the limits. Just as the subject is only represented by the signifier, the object is always representative of the initial radical loss operated by the language. The object dresses itself (or one dresses it) in the promise of a definitive satisfaction, of the mirages of a paradise within reach, but the promise is never kept, the paradise always postponed, and the Sovereign Good never attained. The work of presentation and of "packaging" will always have to be redone....

---

45. Lacan, *Ecrits*, p. 256.

We left in suspense the question of the *relationship of the form* of the fetus which the techniques of the future could bring to birth in different conditions from those that we know. The matter from that time onwards becomes clear at the same time that it becomes impassioned. The relationship of the formal Me is not theoretical but libidinal, we have said. If therefore the,Me is the object of quite considerable investment, if the Me "wanderer" is always ready to absorb the libido which flows back toward him from the objects to which he was previously identified, it is evident that "only that which has human form in comparison, awakens the powerful sentiments which bind man to man, recognized as such at the level of the image".[46] And the question is asked in these works: Will man of the future centuries recognize the product issued from the test tube as a fellow man? This question, we only ask it emphasizing that it is the same that humanity has been asking itself since Adam and Eve.[47] And *Meilleurs des Mondes*

46. L. Beirnaert, "L'avortement est-il infanticide?", in *Études* (Nov. 1970), p. 520.

47. We will only mention here in note form the problem of aggressivity necessarily correlative to narcissism. The former aggression arises from alienation of the lure where the Me is located. The myth of Narcissus, as A. de Waelhens emphasizes, offers the immemorial paradigm of this. The mirror image is loved and hated at the same time. Loved because it is a mirage of unity, hated because it is always fading away: "The subject seeks to do away with his distance from the mirror image, the difference between the other which is the same and the same which is the other. It seeks to coincide. But this can only be done in the destruction of one of the expressions by aggression. But this aggression intrinsically involves the destruction of the other expression. Narcissus, in love with his reflection, throws himself into the water; in so doing he also

or not, the question which remains in suspense, insoluble, is that which Freud asks in *Civilization and its Discontents*, and that which Safouan discusses, "morals of common good which organize themselves entirely around the image of fellowman and the regards which are due to him, lose their hold (I do not say their rights) on the subject which speaks as such, that which would not know how to be constrained to reciprocity... unless he wants to recognize me as his fellow man. Does he want to?"[48]

With this last question which remains open is introduced that of the foundation of ethics and that of the role of "moralist", such that psychoanalysis may speak of it.

All the preceeding permits us to blaze a trail. Psychoanalysis has made us attentive to the question of the relationship of the subject to the signifying chain, and to the status of the lost object, cause of desire.

To recall the existence of a desiring subject, in the elaboration of an ethical speech, supposes the requestioning

---

destroys the mirror image as well as the other self. Is this a self-destruction or a heterodestruction? It is both really since the self is the other and the other is the self." A. de Waehlens, "Rôle de l'aggressivité dans le psychisme humaine" in *Revue theologique de Louvain*, (1973), pp. 159-160. In order to temper the above, we add that the Me, in order to function as the object of love must be declared loveable by the mother. This image of Me which I love then keeps this unknown desire of the Other which has declared me loveable. From that time onwards in the intersubjective meeting there are never two *Identical Me*'s who confront each other. The image of the self marked by the signifier conceals an unknown and remains "open" to a mediation possible by the word.

48. Safouan, *De la structure en psychanalyse*, p. 285.

of morals which take their origin from innate evident principles, known by "L'intellectus principiorum primorum" which
determines the reasonable primate.

To introduce desire into the matter of ethical norms, is
not to replace the anteriority and the principle of reason by
those of the emotional and the psychological. It is to recall, once more, the anteriority of language. For psychoanalysis, morals cannot bring interdicts and obligations in
the name of pure reason. Even the inverse appears: "It is
not reason which founded the moral conscience and its interdicts, it is the interdict which is the foundation of reason.
Moral conscience, indeed, insofar as it calls upon the only
reason (whether it is economical or ideological) is wrong:
its source is in the *incomprehensible limitation imposed by
the irruption of the desire of an other to which is accorded
the same degree of existence as to the self.*"[49]

Therefore reason returns to a third desire which, incomprehensible, comes to break the dual relationship the
existence of which it is quite necessary to recognize. But
this desire expresses itself in a word and the interdict is
primarily an interdict, a language. Also the Law with which
psychoanalysis is concerned is it not that which one may read
in the decalogue, but anterior to the decalogue, there is that
which is conveyed in the word which carries it. For psychoanalysis, the Law is written in no other place besides the
word. It is why, if we may make a remark and open a parenthe-
sis, the Law of laws, that which is the foundation of all laws

49. D. Vasse, *Le Temps du désire*, Paris, Seuil, 1969, p.
136.

cannot be written on stone tablets. These tablets were broken
in the descent from the mountain and the decalogue as we know
it is only man's written transcription, of the Word of "I am",
engraved by fire in the obscure clouds.

The Law, the only Law, that of desire, the Law inscribed
no other place than in the desire, or, if one reverses the
words desire making Law prevents the subject from becoming
one with the signifier.

Beyond all positive legislation, psychoanalysis still
returns to the primate of the signifier, which does not mean
that the conflict is resolved for all that. On the contrary
it is the signifier itself which makes it arise. "No categorical imperative could break the constitutive ambiguity of
desire insofar as the latter is structured according to Oedipus
beyond the limits of the conscience as desire for the mother
imposed by the desire of the father which forbids it. That the
desire is the Law, does not exclude the fact that the inverse
is also true."[50]

So much for the subject and the Law which establishes its
existence. As for the object we have sufficiently insisted on
the possibility that all there was to do was to take the effect
of the metaphor by which the subject is *indicated*, as an object, and to institute the effect of the signified as this
known and accessible object which then takes the name of
Sovereign Good. The known becomes the perverse object. One
may enjoy it and impose this enjoyment on the other for which
one enacts the laws which ought to permit access to it.

---

50. Safouan, *De la structure en psychanalyse*, p. 285.

This way of proceeding, we have said, is a repetition of the formation of the Me, which consists of confusing it in order to be satisfied with the subject of the stated and the subject of the statement.

The temptation exists then to *define* a good or the Good as absolute in order to remove that which is always lacking in this good. The temptation exists to remove the interrogation and the non-knowing, which exist in understanding and the definition of all good, to construct systems and moral syntheses which are not anything but those sutures of which we have spoken, and with which the Me of the moralist may identify.

It is not fruitless to denounce these current practices in the morality of nations and their censors. But can one escape it?[51]

To define a good system, to impose an ideal image of the self on the subject in order that the subject return this image may be the unconscious motive of all moral education. The subject to be moralized must manifest the "qualities" and serve the values of family, nation and race. Does not this attitude, presented with the most laudable motives, call attention to a manipulation more or less disguised?

This said, the moralist no more than the man in the street, can escape from the incessant questioning of praxis and techniques. These techniques come, as do all acts of speech, to requestion synthesis and system which would be solidly established.

---

51. See the excellent book on the subject by Pierre Legendre, *L'amour du censeur. Essai sur l'ordre dogmatique*, Paris, Seuil, 1974.

Language being the condition of desire, desire being the condition of ethical reflection, conflict is inevitable between the subject of the desire and the civilization which welcomes it, between the "personal" and the "social".

Then it is not astonishing that at the end of the congress of which the theme was entitled: *Power of Man over Man, Risks and Limits*, the participants ask the question of their identity. Beyond the object of their discussions, there are other subjects about which philosophers and theologians question each other.

Then who are these theologians?

Are they these passengers of a rocking boat, embarked for an unknown destination and turning round and round having no more than port and starboard as sole landmarks, the polestar being in obscurity? This is the impression which they give the practitioner, practical on the exterior who, engaged in action seems to know the object of his desire, to possess the way which leads toward satisfaction and to know how to answer the questions of why and how.

Facing the certitudes of possession, facing the power of knowledge and the profitability of technology, would a few anguished poets still seek something else, something other in quarreling among themselves in the circle of an apparently sterile phantasm?

Facing the defined, measured, consumable object, re-questioning by their discordant speech the known way of satisfaction within arm's length, would the subjects dare to ask the question of the unnamable and lost object of their unquenched desire.

Facing the unidimensionality of a civilization with paranoiac certitudes, facing a world of the hypertrophied and alienated Me, would men thrown back on their systems,

their convictions and their former quietude, reunite in order
to ask what meaning they should give to their action and to
this civilization to which they belong?

Would they succeed in attaining truth upon truth? One
may doubt it because we know that death alone permits the
attainment of identity with the signifier and most of them
in desiring it prefer to postpone this discovery until later.

Then what is a theologian and what purpose does he serve?

---To transmit a corpus of doctrine?

But this corpus of doctrine thus transmitted, does not it
already have the appearance of a corpse which can only sustain
the feeble inhabitants of the ghetto which find nourishment in
it?

---To rationalize an area defined by faith?

But then this necessary rationalization, is it not the
height of systematic stop gaps, of intolerant manichaeism or
of these hasty sutures which only make secure those who elaborate them?

---To express in reconstructing constantly the master-
piece of his desire which is always unachieved?

Maybe...and beyond all unifying synthesis where his narcissism easily finds its due, the theologian divided subject,
as are all behaviours, a crucified subject desiring to be
recognized in his very division, may become in his Church and
in the world the witness and partner of a humanity in search
of the one who is lost and who for him has the name of God.

His truth, he can find it in the very division, in this
inadequacy within himself, with his world and his objects.
In the beginning is the Word. In the beginning is the conflict....

Roland Sublon

CHAPTER VII

Strategy of a Christian Ethic

*For us morals are a system of realized facts tied
to the total system of the world.*
                                    - Emile Durkheim[1]

*Modernization, whatever elements it implies, is
always a moral and religious problem.*
                                    - Robert N. Bellah[2]

This exposition envisages the power of man over man as *a
moral and religious power*. It examines the fact that the moral
norm is decreed and proposed by certain instances which are
recognized as its custodians and constitute so many social
powers, in this case the Church. It does not deal with the
contents of the norm as such, but with its function.

Churches, and that which concerns us here, the Catholic
Church, indeed present themselves as groups exercising a moral
and religious power, in the midst of society. Briefly said,

----

1. Emile Durkheim, *De la division du travail social*,
Paris, PUF, p. XII.

2. Robert N. Bellah, *Beyond Belief*, (New York, Harper
and Row), 1970, p. 64.

Christianity has implanted an *"ethical system"* into our societies, in which the elements form a coherent whole. The Church offers norms to individuals, it justifies these norms by the Revelation, it diffuses them by its teaching and its preaching, it seeks to control the application of it and to give sanctions in many ways, from moral education to political intervention or the appeal to public opinion.

We will ask ourselves about the *functioning* of such an entirety, insofar as it constitutes *a system of social action*.[3] In the first place, it will consist of an empirical and positive analysis. We are not interested in what the Church should be, but what the Church effectively says and does. It is the beginning of all reflection called "pastoral".[4] We will do it

---

3. We refer to the definition of Max Weber: "By social activity, we mean activity, which from the meaning which was aimed for by the agent and agents, agrees with the behavior of the others, with respect to whom orient its development. (*Economie et Société*, translated from the German, [Paris, Plon, 1971], I, p. 4.)

On the sociology of action and the idea of the system of social action see: Alain Touraine, *Sociologie de l'action*, (Paris, Seuil, 1965). One will find a summary of it in *Encyclopedia Universalis*, under *Action (sociologie de)*.

4. Here we are using the word *pastoral* in its usual sense, such as it is used by Christian communities, and designating the entire actions of the Church. The German authors prefer the expression, *practical theology*, to that of *pastoral theology*.

The word *pastoral* designates a domain but absolutely not a method of reflection. That is the reason for which we prefer for our part to reserve its use for noncritical speech. This supposes elaboration of an analytic and critical reflection of the action of the Church, a science of *praxis ecclesiae* to which corresponds the word praxeology which is less currently used.

with regard to the very theme of the congress: how does the moral and religious power of the Church function in that which concerns the power of man over "life"?

In the second place, this will permit us to direct ourselves toward a *properly faithful interrogation*. This Church calls itself the bearer of Salvation. What is there of Salvation in the Church, if such are the social functions which its action reveal? Between that which the empirical reading will have manifested and that which the second reading invites us to hold, exists a divergence. Is it possible to overcome it and how?[5]

This leads us to envisage a *strategy of moral and religious action for the Church*. By its preaching, Catechism, its educational actions, the Church has diffused and imposed a certain view of man and determined the field of legitimate practices. View and practice are questioned today by the *new possibilities* as much as by new ideologies. The practice of the Church therefore comes to terms with other forms of regulation and other ethical projects. The new possibilities are received against the background of a view of man which has been implanted by centuries of Christianity. Well beyond such and such particular point, it is the very coherence of the ethical system constructed by the Church which is questioned. Is it possible to envisage any criteria of an action which is simultaneously pertinent to social change and contemporary culture and faithful to the Gospel which has been received by the Church?

---

5. For that which concerns the functional, then "believing", "double reading", see J. Audinet, "Quelques problèmes posés par l'analyse de l'action religieuse", in *Social Compass*, XVII (1970), 376.

I. MUTATIONS OF THE CHRISTIAN ETHIC OF LIFE

To describe the changes which affect the diverse aspects
of Christian morality would be an endless task. This, like
the other domains of human existence: religion, social relations, organizations, etc....is caught up in the mutation
which characterizes our time and which one usually designates
by the expression cultural change.

Our purpose therefore, is not to describe it, but to try
to *"understand"* it. *To understand how the Church functions*,
insofar as it is the center of power, in that it concerns the
regulation of morality. Indeed, beyond the anecdotal multiplicity of changes, the renovation of vocabulary, the transformation of intentions and of motivations which animate individuals, and the new language used in teaching, it is possible to detect certain correlations, certain structured arrange-
ments which constitute *the models of functioning.*[6] It seems
as if the Church, in its attempt to adjust its moral teaching
to contemporary cultural change, set to work certain elements,
old or new, in an organized way, according to certain coherent
entities which I call "models". Our hypothesis is that at a
given moment, in a given group, only a limited number of models
exist and that in presenting a new situation one will attempt
to combine them.

----

6. By *model*, I mean the representation of a function
which takes into account relationships between different
elements.

We will propose to analyse the elements of these models, before indicating certain ways in which they can combine.

This work is based on a study of our theme carried out on a collection of catechismal documents. The collection consisted of the following works:

A. *Catéchisme national des diocèses de France* (1947);

B. J. Colomb, *Dieu parmi nous*, (1950), and *Avec le Christ Jésus* (1950);

C. *Le cathéchisme des diocèses d'Allemagne*, French translation (1957);

D. *Fond obligatoire*, CNER (1967).[7]

We will retain three fundamental elements of any system of action:

--- the pursued *aim* and the representation which is given it by the group;

--- the *social tie* in the interior of the group and with other groups in society;

--- *integration* of the individual and the symbolic economy of his identity.[8]

---

7. We limited ourselves to the documents concerning childhood, because from the pedagogical point of view, childhood obliges one to use elementary language, and from the cultural point of view, catechism of children represents the only religious culture of many of our contemporaries. In the domain of this Congress, the first images are fixed by them, from whence comes the interest to analyse them.

It is not possible for us to give the details of our study, but it has furnished the material for this conference.

8. Cf. *Les principes de mouvements sociaux d'après Touraine*, in Guy Rocher, *Le changement social*, 3, (Paris, HMH, 1968), p. 148.

1. *From an Ethic of the Nature of Life, to an Ethic of the Dynamics of Life*

In order to act, an actor sets himself certain aims, which take place and meaning in a view of the world, and by dint of these become motivating. One of the aspects of preaching and of moral catechism of the Church consists precisely in proposing and rendering legitimate some perspectives which are the foundation of moral action. To come to our point, the Church offers an image of life which justifies the ethical requests formulated to its purpose. This image of life is changing.

Two things in the current catechism characterize this change: in the first place, *the vocabulary of life takes a more and more important place* in the teaching of the Church, but in the second place, and simultaneously, *it empties itself of its precise content.*

The classic catechism devotes a certain number of chapters to the *respect for life.* Life means the bodily life of man and that which is permitted and forbidden in this regard is determined in a precise way: murder, suicide, etc....are forbidden because they run contrary to the respect for life. This bodily life is situated in an entirety. Man takes his place in a hierarchy of beings, at the summit of which is God the Creator. Life comes from him (who has no body). Man participates in the divine life, with his soul, elevated to supernatural life. These "two lives", in the words of the old catechisms, define the place of man in the entirety of reality, natural and supernatural.

This entirety is ordered and hierarchical. It is a cosmology at the same time as an order of salvation. The one and the other reinforce each other. It is the order of visible

things which in some way founds and guaranties that of the
invisible things. Inversely it is the order of invisible
realities which gives grandeur to the visible realities and
in particular to man.[9]

From that time onwards human action takes place in this
order. It is not so much what one will call later the respect of the person which establishes the interdicts concerning life (death or sexuality), as the fact that only the acts
which follow the lines of order are justified, order which is
simultaneously *a cosmic order and a divine order*. "Life is
sacred", life comes from God, "life escapes the power of
man."[10]

---

9. Cf. Document A, ch. 57, p. 193-195, the 5th Commandment: "Thou Shalt Not Kill", "The Respect of Life". The Commandments are related to God the Creator.
    Document B, "That which explains all is the love of
God" (p. 38); "God made the body of man; All is for man; the
spirit must command and not the body; the body is a dangerous
servant; it is necessary to respect the body of man" (p. 310).
    Document C, "God gave us a body and life, likewise
our physical and spiritual capacities. He has organized and
given life to our body by our soul" (p. 333).
    Document D, "God calls to him the total man, soul and
body, which are really one" (p. 97).
    One sees the progression: A affirms Divine order, in
the sense of commandment, a general way to divine order, har-
mony of created beings. B and C explain this order for man
related through the intention of the love of God and the spiritual faculties. In D, all mention of an order has disappeared:
the sole mention made of the body and soul is made only to
challenge the duality which one supposes is implied in such
categories. One passes from the order of the law and nature
to the order of the economy of salvation, then to the individual called by God, but not situated.

10. One will take note of the vocabulary. It concerns the
"respect" of the body (A and B), "honoring the body" (C).

The only initiative possible is that which follows this
order. "All attainment of life is of itself sin." The great
duty is to "conserve life" and to "suppress obstacles which
are injurious to health".[11] The only exceptional cases would
be those required by the good of the superior order (such as
justified defense of martyrdom).[12]

This ample vision is indistinct in *recent documents*. The
word "life" is no longer used there as order and nature, but
as *dynamism and value*. The precise chapters concerning the
respect for life and definite indications in this regard have
disappeared. On the other hand, the vocabulary of life has
invaded all of the catechism: but it no longer designates the
bodily life of the supernatural life. Life is everything which
is in the field of man, that which he can animate and trans-
form, everything with which he may construct his human world.
From whence comes the importance attached to the social and
relational aspects of this "life"? The word is no longer

---

11. Documents A, B, and C indicate the precise manner in
which things are forbidden and allowed. Thus A, p. 194: "It
is sometimes permitted to kill: 1) for punishing a criminal
condemned by a court; 2) in order to defend one's country
against the enemy; 3) in order to defend oneself against an
evildoer; when one cannot safeguard life any other way."
There is a question concerning suicide and another
concerning the suffering of animals.

12. In the traditional catechism is joined to the 5th
Commandment that which may equally be injurious to the life
of the soul: A deals with a question on scandal (p. 194); C
joins to the 5th Commandment the chapters concerning: the
body and the after life, spiritual aptitudes and faculties,
the concern for our eternal salvation and for eternal salvation of our fellowmen (p. 114-119).

associated with nature or the body but with an event and
group.[13]

Simultaneously, the vision of an order disappears. Life
is situated henceforth in the register of *desire*, of *attitude*
and of *meaning*. For the cosmic order is substituted a *historical development* in which man is the initiator. It no
longer consists of a sacred universe, exterior to man and
which includes him, but a secular construction site in which
he is a worker.

However, oddly enough, the job is not defined. All precision concerning obligations or interdicts disappears in the
recent catechism. One will say it is a question of elaborating a new relationship--faith and life. But whereas in the
preceeding perspectives, this was assured by the mediation
of the order of beings, and indicated by an explicit moral
law and casuistic precision which sprang from it, the life-
faith relationship is henceforth dependent on the intention
and action of individuals.[14]

---

13. D, p. 99: "In a world which will never be perfect,
men can undertake efforts in order that there may be more joy
there, more love, more peace. Certainly, evil comes to con-
tradict these efforts, above all the evil which comes from
sinful men, but the union of men and the witness of Christians
will bring to those who suffer, hope which gives meaning to
life and which is a perpetual source of concrete efforts."
One perceives the displacement. No longer an order
inspiring precise behaviour, but rather attitudes with respect to human relationships. All precise teaching on the
body has disappeared from document D, just as all precision
concerning the physical life of man.

14. D, p. 31: "Catechism must not dissociate faith and
life. It must learn to recognize the Christian meaning of the

But intention and action are conceived in terms of value
and of meaning; not at all in technical or practical terms.
Although one could say that *the way in which life is presented*
in certain forms of recent teaching *is precisely that which
renders impossible an ethic of life* such as discoveries required.

Rather than emphasizing the alternative, either ancient
cosmology or the rejection of a cosmology to the benefit of
subjectivity, would it not be a question of elaboration of a
new vision of the world which may make the foundation for the
action of man? Vision which would no longer be that of the
order of nature or of the dynamics of values, but that of man
in his relationship to cosmic and social reality, practitioner
and technician of his own transformation, including his ethical
transformation.

2. *From Conformity to Social Order, to Creative Initiative*

Any actor finds himself in a network of social ties which
determine the adherence to his group and his position with respect to other groups. One of the aspects of moral education
given by the Church was to secure social ties and to make them
function, assuring the identity of the group, and the behavior
of the individuals. Human existence is the concern of the

---

values of daily life and the Christian meaning of his own spiritual experience. The child may at least find a way to grow
nearer to the Word of God. He may even find real signs for
his faith. This exercise of "reading the signs" of current
life constitutes one of the essential orientations of the
catechism."

group, as well as the concern of the individual. In the domain which holds our attention, this is the position of the mechanisms of education and social control, which are also in a state of change.

At the outset, in the classical catechisms, the order in which the action of the Christian was outlined was a social order at the same time as a cosmic order. Cosmic order, social order, ecclesiastical order went on equal footing. The key idea here is that of "power". The same power of God guaranteed the order of the world and the authority of the Church. As an indication: the vocabulary is the same concerning creation, life and the ministerial authority of the Church. "God has power over everything and the Church has received power from God to teach and govern the faithful."[15]

This affirmation corresponded to *an extention of power of the Church*. This power could intervene in all domains including that which was not strictly of the supernatural order. Society and the Church had the same boundaries. The Church had the recognized social function of expressing the moral order of society, and this not only in the name of salvation, but in the name of "natural law". In this sense no actual or possible domain escaped its jurisdiction.[16]

---

15. A, p. 70.

16. The doctrine of the Church, "guardian by the will of God and by the mandate of Christ, of the natural and supernatural order" (Pie XII, Com sempre, Noel 1942 in Marmy Documents, no. 747), is found in the very structure of the catechisms. Thus it is around the idea of order that the document presents a teaching concerning the family, the state, the superiors, the international community (p. 319-330).

Such a power corresponded to *the modes of intervention*. Without analysing them in detail, let us say that the Church had at its disposal an adequate mechanism and a body of experts--moralists--whose job it was to explain the common doctrine and to envisage its application to new situations. From the point of view of the simple Christian, he relied on this "doctrine of the Church". In unforeseen circumstances, he knew that he must wait for the Church to speak, or he could consult and put to work the hierarchy of knowledge-power which was that of the experts, so to assure the rectitude of his judgment and the conformity of his behaviour.

A double déplacement is produced, concerning each of these points. As far as the extent of the power of the Church is concerned, the Church is no longer perceived as covering the totality of social space. The Church's way of speaking of itself indicates this.[17] It has become in pluralist societies, as ours, one group among others which, by the initiative of the "mission", of evangelizing, tries to diffuse the Gospel. But it is no longer possible for the Church from that time onwards to speak in the name of totality and in an exclusive way. Other possibilities exist, other ideologies circulate in the field of information of the society. It is no longer the universal order which it may invoke, rather the particular point of view of believers, either in order to show that it reunites the human, similar to it and accomplishes it, or in

---

17. Cf. Raymond Facélina, *Témoignage de la foi en Dieu dans le monde contemporaine*, Strasbourg, CERDIC, 1973, which presents an analysis of missiologic vocabulary.

order to break with it in the name of Christian singularity.[18]

In the domain which occupies us, interventions of the
authority of the Church, according to the moments and objects,
take one or another way. The themes brought into play vacillate between natural law and the Gospel, between the word for
all men and the word for the Christians.

Simultaneously *the modes of intervention* of authority are
no longer received in the same way. Precisely in the moral
domain and particularly in that which concerns the power of
man over life, the insistence on the attitude of responsibility and of significant action involves the individual's consciousness of his responsibility but also of his freedom.
That which appeared to be of "value" previously: submission
to authority, tends to be perceived as resignation, indeed
alienation.[19] Who can say what is moral action and where the
origin of the moral action is located? The expert as the man
of authority is challenged while the claim for each one to be
fully responsible and to decide on his own action is shaped.

The adjustable double deplacement, day after day, in the
interventions and multiple situations, leads one to formulate

18. Cf. J. Audinet, "Agir Pastoral et Révélation", in
Révélation de Dieu et langage des hommes, (Paris, Cerf, 1972),
p. 11-33.

19. The thing is perceptible in recent documents. The
mutation of themes concerning the catechism of the Church is
an indication thereof, as is the fear manifested by the catechists involving an authority qualified as "justified": Vg.
D, p. 33: "One will avoid a legalist observance and one will
open the perspective of filial and fraternal life which the
beatitudes evoke."

the following hypothesis: *that which has vitalized the Church group and has permitted the return to it of an identity within social change and contemporary culture is what puts it in danger of disintegration today.* The claim of responsibility and liberty is made just as strongly as the image of authority was encrusted by the centuries of power of the Church. But it leads beyond to the disintegration of the group, if the collective dimension of interpersonal bond is not taken into account. Inversely, to want to restore the old mechanisms of functioning and to act as if the Church still expressed the common social consensus, or as if the interventions of authority were received without debate, would lead to the same result. The question asked here is that of new forms of organization and diffusion of the message of the Church in a social pluralist whole, and of new ways to conceive the relationship of freedom and authority.[20]

3. *The Individual: Identity and Freedom*

By dint of action, and specifically by moral action, the individual finds and reinforces his identity. He identifies himself with the group and with his goals by dint of the game of *symbolic economy* which assures both his autonomy and his relationships with others. Let us make note of two indications of change in the system of Christian ethics:

Security: That which involves life is for the individual the place of the flowering and the source of anguish. The role

---

20. Cf. Gérard Defois, *Le Pouvoir dans l'Eglise*, (Paris, Cerf, 1973).

of religion in all society will be to channel anguish at the same time as indicating "the way of life". The old catechisms offered a "portrait of the Christian" which corresponded to the portrait of the honest man, that is to say, the man integrated into society. Based on this premise, all of the man's actions were situated and fixed in a sort of "topography" where the good and bad routes were indicated in advance. To follow the way of life was not only to assure the tranquility of the soul, but also the gratifications which were attached to it, either social recognition in the here and now, or in the hereafter. To have oneself depart from this pattern was to find anguish and incur "the shame of sin". [21]

The Church offered to the individual a "symbolic order" where he could unfold his existence. One often risks caricaturing it and not seeing that through traditional preaching concerning the morality of finalities just as by the function of the sacraments, notably that of penitence, individual masses have discovered a refinement of the conscience, a greater sense of responsibilities, an opening on the absolute and universal which has channeled their anguish and given sense to their

---

21. The vocabulary of shame exists in A and C, having to do with imperfect contrition, A, p. 131, C, p. 231. About the body the symbolism used is that of danger and combat in C and B. Thus C, p. 135, (Book of the Master): "You see that it is dangerous to always listen to one's body, to give it that which it demands. It is often necessary to deny its requests. It is the body's responsibility to obey our spiritual soul. One must learn how to deprive oneself, to content oneself with that which is useful, to make an effort...."
Let us remember that the vocabulary of shame is for Durkheim one of the indications of a non-differentiated society (o.c., p. 56).

lives, that is to say, an inroad by and into Christian symbolism.

However, *the cost of the operation* (second indication) was considerable. The autonomy of the individual was secured by his conformity with the group, but no departures and no grasp of distance with respect to the constraints of the group were tolerated. Constraint overtook the individual most intimately: his conscience, which in case of conflict often sacrificed the individual to the group. In the area which concerns us, interdicts on life have long designated--and continue to designate Christians--as "apart". The interrogations and questionings have considerably effective charge, precisely because beyond such and such a particular point, it is the whole of a symbolic order--and by the same token, the identity of individuals and their security--which is attacked.

In the face of the great implications which issued from liberal thinking or the ideologies of liberation, the preaching of the Church has reacted.[22] The themes of "choice", of "freedom", of "personal conscience" take a privileged place in the catechism. The themes of the "law" and of the "commandment", indeed "of sin" and of "penitence", not to speak

---

22. From the historical point of view, the study of B. Groethuysen, *Origines de l'esprit bourgeois en France*, Paris, NRF, 1927, shows how, with the advent of the new independent class which is the Bourgeoisie, the preaching of the 18th century reinforced the symbolic themes of the power of God, of judgment, of sin and hell. But such preaching only served to reinforce the indifference of the new class rising to power. Cf. equally the work of Elisabeth Germain, *La Catéchèse du Salut dans la France de la Restauration*, (Paris, Beauchesne, 1968) and *Langages de la foi à travers l'histoire*, (Paris, Fayard, 1972).

of "last days" blur and sometimes disappear. *It all seems as if the points of reference of the traditional symbolism were left in the shadows to the benefit of the anthropological themes which are less vulnerable and more contemporary.*

In the mind of many preachers one does not exclude the other. To start with man leads to the mystery of God. However the risk is great, of stopping en route and to substitute for a symbolic entirety new ideologies under the cover of Christianity.[23] The cost of the operation is then considerable. The anguish is no longer that of constraint, but that of solitude and the unknown.

We find ourselves, in sum, in the following situation: in an old symbolic order which is moral, social and religious, but which no longer functions. Partial essays which attempt to propose a new Christian view of existence, but with the risk of leaving aside one of the essential aspects of a religious morality: that which implants it in individuals, knowledge of the fact that it offers a symbolic economy of existence.

4. *Conclusion of the First Part: The Ethics as a System of Action*

We have tried to understand the actual mutation of the Christian ethics from the point of view of its function and

---

23. Cf. Gérard Defois, *Les risques du langage croyant,* in *Catéchèse,* no. 52, July 1973, p. 335-350.

according to three elements: view of the world, social bond, and identity of the individual.

It would be possible to formalize relationships between these different elements and *to construct models*, taking into account the function of the ethic. We have not done this in order that this exposé should not be too austere. We will briefly indicate in the tables how these models present themselves.[24]

	MODEL 1	MODEL 2
World View	Order (creation and supernatural) Life: Natural supernatural	Interpersonal relationships and history Life: Relational
Social Bond	Coextensive Church the society Power: -hierarchical -organized -universal	Church: particular group Power: -multiple -partial
Identity and Action of the Individual	Obedience -conformity -determination	Belonging -initiative -invention

---

24. The table above tries to formalize the models of Christain ethics as a system of action, as they emerge from the preceeding analysis. One will note:

1) Formally the two are mutually exclusive. Actually many speeches or behaviors try to combine them.

Two remarks:

---*a model never exists in a pure state.* But the elaboration of formal models allows realization of the coherence and noncoherence of a concrete situation.

---one may envisage all concrete situations as a *combination of diverse models.* By this even, such an analysis brings out neurological points which are not immediately apparent and on which depend the function of the action.

To speak of the power of man over man and in particular over life of man takes on different meanings according to the predominant model of action in a situation. The words "life", "freedom", "power", do not function in the same way. To envisage a *"strategy of a Christian ethics"* in contemporary society would not only be a case of reflection on "that which must be, but equally an *enterprise* with a view to transforming that which exists.

For example in trying to combine them in a sort of synchretic speech.

Or even in making a table of them on a vision of the world (II) for reinforcing a sociality (I) or behaviors (I).

Or inversely now the Model I for that which concerns the world view and the ecclesiastical bond, in taking Model II in action. One might pursue this combination.

2) To formalize these models allows the seizure of *the points of difficulty*: Model II offers nothing as to the new relationship to the cosmos. It invites one to consider the question of power otherwise. It risks only offering an ideology of freedom and initiative and not determinations.

3) *Research* might precisely attach itself to these points in such a way as to offer other models of functioning. In this the Church may be a place of invention of new models of social function and behavior.

Our second part tries to indicate a few criteria for such an enterprise.

II. PROPOSITIONS

1. *What is it Possible to Do?*

Such a question does *not call for a general answer*. The analysis has disclosed a plurality of vision, discrepancies between the teaching of authority and the initiative of individuals, symbolic mutations which are so many elements of the Christian ethical system in mutation. The general considerations would be negation of that which the analysis disclosed. We are rather invited to wonder about the possible actions having to do with each element and their interrelationship. *If things happen thus, who may intervene? How, in the name of what?*

It should be observed that to refrain from intervening *is equally an illusion*. Whether it wishes it or not, and whatever certain members may think, the Church in our society appears to be one of the principle centers of reference and power concerning ethics. To refuse this role, would be to lie to reality? But as for all the great social powers issued from preceeding epochs, it is incumbent on it to assure the transformation of its role.

But act in the name of what? The pastor, like all responsible men in the Church and all Christians, knows that the Church *is the bearer of a Salvation*. It is bearer of a Gospel

from which it receives its power, but a Gospel which also
judges this power. Functional analysis discloses the language,
social mechanisms, symbolical functions by which the given
groups manifest that of which the Church is the bearer. It
takes into account the way in which the particular groups
refer to what they have received, without taking into account
this "ultimate reality" which escapes all analysis. Even by
this it can open other possibilities, and permit to "shift"
the questions and interventions.

In this sense a strategy cannot be deduced purely and
simply from functional analysis. Action puts into play more
than the mechanisms of action. It is why the "functional
reading" returns to a "faithful reading" which is normally
the work of a theology.

We will try, in reconsidering each one of the points
analyzed above, to indicate the possibilities of action at the
same time as to sketch that which they may indicate for a theology which would wish to be a "theory of ecclesiastical practice".

2. *From Discourse on Man to Discourse of Man*

All moral action is registered in a vision of the world.
It implies a word which gives sense. It is the relationship
of the word to action which is the question here.

At the level of concrete practice we focused on the two
great systems to which today Christian morals refer: a vision
of cosmic order, another of the personal and historic type.
Let us recognize that it is difficult for us to make a place
for "practical" and "technical" discourse, that is to say for

a discourse elaborating from an experimented and verified action, whether it concerns the biological, social or political domain. This is often either purely ignored, or given a definite meaning beforehand.[25]

Is an *inverse approach* possible, that is, an approach which is not a repetition of the old meaning established by another way, but allowing the introduction of a possible meaning? Certain groups attempt this today, but this presupposes certain conditions.

The point of departure of such an approach is the action, but also the established meanings. These would not intervene only as answers in which it is a question of furnishing new situations, but as object of a question, a critic destined to establish their pertinence (relevance). In this sense to speak is neither to repeat an instituted discourse, nor to risk spontaneous discourse, but it is to try to elaborate a word having a meaning from experience. *The possibilities of meaning rather than saying "the" meaning.*

This renders an instituted discourse or discourses all the more necessary, such as they come to us from the Tradition. Through their words of which we saw the misadventures, something essential is said, but it is a question of saying it otherwise. From this time onwards a moral education is not the absence of moral discourse, but quite the contrary: apprenticeship starting from what has been said, and of which

---

25. It is notable that, in the analyzed documents, each time an allusion is made to a "practice" or to a "work", these are immediately reinterpreted in terms of attitudes, and signification, telescoping, even the technique and operation of all human practice.

one seeks to manifest the pertinence, to say, in other words,
something pertinent today. In that which concerns life, for
example, one may not purely and simply challenge the ancient
cosmology, any more than one may take it as it is. But what
was said there about an ordered creation is the bearer of
something that it is necessary for us to try to explain otherwise.[26]

To be thus attentive to the discourse "making itself",
and not only to rephrase prepared discourses, opens the door
to *multiple provisory discourses*. This is already the factual
situation. It appears often as if legitimate, when it is
doubtless the condition of survival. But if one does not
want to dream, to what extent is this possible, either from
the point of view of the individuals, or from the point of
view of social control of the group, or from the point of view
of what the Church is bearer?

From the point of view of individuals the question is
this: with whom is such an approach possible?

Traditionally, the distinction between majors and minors
allows us to differentiate between popular teaching and learned
discourse, even if little by little the learned discourse has
invaded popular teaching. The ladder of culture and the ladder
of power are reunited. The diffusion of information coupled
with the fact that religious culture and secular culture are
no longer on a par breaks down such a distinction.

However levels still exist and it would be worth the
trouble to distinguish between research in morals and its

---

26. Cf. Defois, *Les risques du langage croyant, loc. cit.*

cultural diffusion. The work concerning the production and
the diffusion of religious discourse scarcely begins and the
declarations on the means of information have scarcely undertaken to put technology to work in this domain. Charisma and
ideology still remind one of the gravity of communication which
would offer to each man the accessible elements of information
and the means of really deciding freely.[27]

In the present confusion, such a strategy would correspond
to the role of "educator" which the Church recognizes for itself. The "service of man" implies certain conditions concerning information and education if one does not want to earn the
words; *to educate for change* and not only to proclaim it.

3. *Unity of the "Faith" and Moral Behaviors*

That which makes the strength of the Catholic group is
that in the name of the same faith the same behaviors were imposed, at least theoretically, on the members of the Church.
Moreover this passed much beyond the regulation of morality,
since it was the same thing within the liturgical domain, for
example. We are caught today between ancient monolithism and
the breaking up of the group which seems the very consequence
of renewal. Is it possible to imagine other forms of social
regulation which could assure a unity without diversity bringing disintegration.

---

27. Concerning the diffusion of religious discourse, cf.
Jean Rémy, "Opinion publique, groupes de pression et autorité
constituée dans l'Eglise Catholique", in *Social Compass*, XIX
(1972), 155-184.

Two points seem to arise here:

----First of all *the conception of unity*: this was conceived as the total system of the world. Unity was the equiv-
alent of universality. In moral practice of former times the
fasting on Friday had as much importance as the profession of
faith.

In certain areas, for example, in political practice, a
certain pluralism begins to be recognized. What can it be,
for example, where the power of man over his body is concerned?

----This brings up another point: *the distinction between
faith and morals*. Personal and kerygmatic "morals" reanimated
the Christian moral edifice in showing how all moral behavior,
such as is expressed by the Church, is bound up in the mystery
of Salvation. But even here they began its disintegration,
because in repudiating the ancient cosmology it was not possible for them to establish the unity of moral action otherwise
than by an explicit and personal approach which is not the
social prerogative of all. If in the Christian universe, the
foundations of morals--faith--came from the self, it is no
longer the same. Socially, morals which emanated from Christianity are more widespread than the explicit faith.

To turn back to the confessing community risks being a
flight which evades the problem, because such a community cannot make an abstraction of either the historical ties of Christianity and of our society, or the present witness. From this
point onwards, the Church as a group cannot avoid *announcing
in the name of what it makes such and such a demand*. It is a
work of purification of Christian morality which aims at not
making the Church say what it does not say. The Christian
root is often buried under the branches it has engendered,
and more than ever our contemporaries are sensitive to the

critical truth with relation to themselves. The disputing
force of the Gospel must be initiated by the Church. This
will avoid the equivocation of a Christian group having
nostalgia for the past, or seeking something novel; but
rather, in the name of the identity of the faith it has to
take note of the requirements which seem to be essential
for manifesting its specificity. No longer will it be a
total discourse or a discourse universal in meaning, but a
discourse of the *Christian difference*, attesting that which
this group bears among the other human groups.

But at the same time, *the acceptance of the diversities
of fact, which are to be judged, not literally, but by the
criteria of the evangelical spirit. It is therefore less a
question of deciding on behavior than to offer criteria* to
those who want to appeal to the Gospel, in the present situation.

4. *The Agents of Moral Regulation*

The diffusion of the moral teaching of the Church and the
regulation of morals were secured by the organization of the
Church. This terrain is cross-ruled by the permanents of the
Church, the clergy, who in fact had been considered as much
guardians of morals as ministers of sacraments or of the word.
The traditional pastoral-letter, in its pedagogical framework,
narrowly overlapped the diverse aspects of the role of the
"priest". By this means the task was precise, the verification easy, there was no discrepancy between the education received at the seminary and action in the field. It was a question of reproducing in the field, with good sense, that which

the cleric had learned, and we have seen that the pyramid of power concerning the specialists corresponded with the pyramid of knowledge concerning ethics.[28]

Ecclesiastical organization no longer exists by itself. Other systems of reference exist, as do other organizations of education, and another relationship to experience: an ethic of fact which before any discourse attempts some adjustments, often at an exorbitant price. How can the organization of the Church envisage being situated in such surroundings?

Even at the bosom of the Church, distinctions are taking shape; the role of the preacher or of catechist is not that of the moralist. If the thing were easy to say, it is difficult to make it work. In fact the catechist or the preacher is often the tributary of "ordinary discourse" and elaborate provisions by the specialists. The Christian community is the point of departure and arrival for all word in the Church. In fact often the communities reproduce and appropriate that which has been said elsewhere. Although it affirms the contrary, the ancient system of diffusion continues to function. This, doubtless, cannot be avoided, but emphasizes the importance of the collaboration and the communication between practitioners: catechists and preachers and specialists.[29]

---

28. One may recall the ambiguous origins of the pastoral theology of which the aim was "to form a functional clergy, in the framework of a Catholic state". Cf. P. A. Liege, "Positions de la Théologie pastorale", in *Le Point Théologique*, 1, (Paris, Beauchesne, 1971), p. 54.

29. Cf. J. Audinet, "Questions de Méthode en Théologie Pastoral", in *Le Point Théologique*, 1, p. 73-89.

On a larger scale, to pose the question of the regulation
of morals from the point of view of cultural models according
to which it is accomplished seems to me must lead us to make
precise the role of the dogmatist, as that of the moralist,
and the scientist, and to ask ourselves about the forms of
collaboration with the diverse instances of society in grips
with moral cultural and contemporary religious change. One
has had a tendancy to connect the morals to theology, in order
to depart from the old distinctions. This has its opposite
which is to leave the specifics of ethical problems in the
shadows. On the other hand, if one admits that the Church has
a specific role concerning the morals in our society; at least
in fact, from this point onward, it is no longer possible for
the Church to exercise this alone. One would wish that there
were actual *"laboratories"* where each one according to his
role could elaborate a strategy of moral action and teaching
corresponding to the social mutation which is ours. Millions
of people have confidence in the Church. The price to pay is
too much for her not to take, in the name of faith, the initiative of a liberation of morals.

CONCLUSION

In making our way, we have touched on many theoretical
questions. Let us mention simply: the relationship between
revelation and morals, faith and the sacred, the believing
group and the institution, science and faith, etc.....Our
purpose was to show that such questions, if they are the

object of the necessary theoretical studies, are also questions which one may tackle differently: from the point of view of the functioning of human groups. From this point of view the consequences of such an affirmation or such a stance are paid for always with a human price. "It is necessary for us to make a morality," said Durkheim, but he added: "One fact does not change in a turn of the hand, even if it is desirable."[30] Present scientific, social and political mutations are also religious. How is it possible for those who appeal to the Gospel to elaborate a strategy of their social action which carries within it the liberation of the faith?

Jacques Audinet

---

30.   Emile Durkheim, *op. cit.*, p. XII.

CHAPTER VIII

The Power of Man over Man

Having been invited by the organizers of the congress of
Strasbourg, professor F. Böckle of Bonn came intending to present six theses on one aspect of the power of man over man.
When on the eve of his address, Mr. Böckle was urgently called
home, he charged Mr. Korff, professor at Tübingen to set forth
and explain what he would have said to us.

The text which we publish below therefore comprises two
distinct elements: on one hand the simple statements of the
six theses of M. Böckle, on the other hand the commentary made
by Mr. Korff at Strasbourg, which was subsequently reviewed
and approved by Mr. Böckle.

The statements of the theses of Mr. Böckle are introduced
in italics by the following marginal numbers: 1, 1.1, 1.2,
1.3, 2, 2.1, 2.2, 2.3, 3, 3.1, 3.2, 4, 4.1, 4.2, 4.3, 5, and
6. Each statement is immediately followed by a commentary by
Mr. Korff.

This first text is completed by a short communication
from Professor B. Schüller of Bochum, on the distinction between deontological norms and teleological norms: it is indeed in the interest of avoiding a premature interpretation
which the reader could make of the quotation of Mr. Schüller,
that is in the statement 2.2 of Mr. Böckle.

1. *"The elaboration and the proclamation of moral norms in themselves establish a specific form of the power of man over man."*

Ethics organizes man by means of norms. Such a radicality makes it clear that wondering about the morality of a possible power over man cannot be reduced to wondering about the choice of means, *which would be from the outside, that is to say, "technical"*, in the broadest sense of the word, but that above everything else it brings one back to wondering about the structure of the power which is held by the ethic itself. The specific structure of power of ethics is comprised only of norms. Norms prove to be the products of man, the regulators of his activities of interpretation, organization and structuralization, and the moral reasoning which is expressed in them is not guaranteed by the single fact that the individual accepts them and obeys them effectively; that he submits to them. This moral reasoning must be by its very essence, measured by its capacity to help man to be fully man by liberating himself. Consequently, even ethical norms may be elaborated and utilized in a manipulative way and, in this case, can be denounced as such.

But where to find the criteria, permitting the elaboration and use of the norms, in such a way as to help man to become fully himself? This question is the true pivot of all of these theses of Mr. Böckle which one is proposing to interpret, and in the course of which Mr. Böckle reveals as directional values, essentially two fundamental criteria, which he then applies to the diverse aspects of the problem of norms, at the basic level as well as at the level of application. The first, the *criterion of transparency*, is stated in the thesis 1.3: "In view of their normative character for moral behavior, the norms must in principle, be without ambiguity (= transparent). Insofar as they are transparent, they lose their manipulative character."

The second, which I would like to call the *criterion of the conditional*, is developed in theses 2 to 4. According to this criterion, the fundamentally conditional, relational and hypothetical character of moral prescriptions (if only these conform to their prescribed contents and are synthetic, and immediate regulators of concrete human action) must be preserved intact according to the executive phase of its imperative claim. All attempts which would aim, in the intention of preserving the validity of norms on an ill-conceived foundation, to deny the conditional character of the requirement expressed by these norms, and to "hypostate" this requirement in total absolute value, would necessarily involve manipulation. This would lead, indeed, to the edification of a pantheon of moral principles which blindly govern man. The norms, to transpose a biblical word, are made for man, and not man for the norms.

Moreover, these two criteria are simultaneously a great help to us in understanding the proper development of the argumentation in the theses of Mr. Böckle, development of which we shall indicate, summarily at first, the principle phases.

Theses 1 and 2, before examining all the possible implications, are concerned with revealing, above all, the two cited criteria, thanks to which the claiming of the power of ethical norms must be rid of all suspicion of manipulation and guaranteed in its non-manipulative character.

Theses 2 completes this first point, adding that these criteria, precisely, lose nothing of their imperative and

directional value for ethics, even in the hypothesis where the
unconditional character of requirement expressed by the norms,
can only finally be based in the perspective of a theonomy.

Thesis 3 applies this to the transmission of norms by the
Church and the question of their confirmation by the Magisterium.

It is only now that the way is open, in principle, to
ethical judgment on the real domain of means, that is to say,
on the numerous purely technical possibilities of power of man
over man: the means are exempt of all manipulation--and this
is the kernel of thesis 4--insofar as the norms governing them
are not themselves used in a manipulative way.

The logical continuation is the emphasis, in thesis 5, on
the revealed ethical problematics, with the sociological background of the concrete mechanisms of power. Thanks to this
problem in thesis 6, finally, one applies a critical rule to
the real pretentions of authority normative for those who hold
the political or moral power, in sum for all directors and
manipulators.

1.1 *Norms are moral directives, regulating concrete
human action in an obligatory but only general manner."*

What does this mean: "regulating in an obligatory but
only general manner"? In this regard, Böckle writes in his
article, *Infallible Norms?*: "regulating in a general way
means...in itself neither to regulate equally (universally)
for all time, nor to regulate in such a way that such behavior should, independent of all possible circumstance,
therefore without any exception (absolutely), be considered
as ordered or forbidden. This does not prevent one from
elaborating on ethical statements which are valid without

exception and which determine the action in an obligatory way in each case. But what are these statements? In the first place, without any doubt, all these imperatives have an analytic and tautological character. "You will not act unjustly, you will not kill unjustly" etc....signifies in a different form, nothing other than "to kill unjustly is always unjust". Such tautologies are certainly evident and absolute, but they do not constitute regulations for concrete action.[1] We would like to know what this means concretely in each case: not to act unjustly, not to kill unjustly, etc.....To similar questions and to analogous questions, ethics cannot bring any universally obligatory response, nor of value without exception, since the possible ethical statements expressing an absolute demand, remain so formal that they do not immediately present themselves as regulatory values. But inversely it must be said that ethical statements which, by their concrete character, are effectively regulators of action, lose nothing of their reasonable normalcy, even if they are not of absolute or universal import. They have their own logical normative structure giving access to a human power-to-be, which is a suitable starting point.[2] The *duration* and the *diffusion* of a norm are the circumstantial concomitant values, but do not constitute its validity. For internal verity and the rationality of a norm, it is of little importance, to speak as

------

1. F. Böckle, "Des Normes Infaillibles?" in H. Küng (ed.), *Fehlbar?* Zürich, Benziger, 1973, p. 293.

2. On that which follows cf. W. Korff, *Norme et moralité, Etudes sur la logique de la raison normative*, Mayence, 1973, p. 65ff.

Pascal; that it is only valid on this side of the Pyrenées or
beyond; that it was approved yesterday or only today; that it
ceases, should the occasion arise, to exist tomorrow. The
only decisive thing is this coherence which is everywhere and
always undeniable and convincing; by which the norm proves its
rationality to the subject, in the frame of its own horizon of
knowledge, and imposes itself on him as obligatory. Consequently, it seems totally aberrant to want to determine the
validity of a norm from the quantitative givens of its diffusion and its duration. Because, even if it is demonstrated
that a norm is equally valuable for all cultures and epochs,
which seems to be the case for the forbidding of incest in
spite of a vast sample of variants, it is not precisely the
diffusion, nor the duration as such which prove its rationality but rather the agreed coherence of a network of conflict-
ing motives. Though crystallizing normally until this time,
this network is however submitted to important variations with
regard to forms of legitimization, and the range and the speci-
fication of its contents. These motives which, for their part,
have always assured the value of norms and will certainly assure it in the future, must doubtlessly furnish well grounded
arguments of contents and of logical structure.

This certainly does not exclude that concomitant criteria,
such as duration and diffusion, which manifest themselves in
multiple quantitative variants, in spite of everything are unable to reclothe with great importance certain processes of the
establishment and of legitimization of norms. As a general
rule, it is often the case that an indisputably viable norm is
based on justifications of such complexity and variety that it
goes beyond the reason of the individual and makes him take as
sufficiently precise legitimization these concomitant criteria

and not that on which they are actually grounded. The real problem of this evasion in favor of secondary aspects, which is naturally suited for a fundamental attitude oriented by tradition and directed from the exterior, only appears when new situations arise; when one perceives new motivations. The crisis of the viable norm attains the one who follows it and who, in these conditions, reacts to all novelty in fear of having to separate from that which exists, by resistance to all apprenticeship and by a desire for immobility.

But a specifically revolutionary position, which takes the exact counterpart of this extreme position and radically refuses all reference to tradition and all direction from the exterior does not constitute the only possible alternative, nor even that which would be predominant. The latter position is rather defined by a fundamental attitude which starts from this conviction: that a viable, transmitted, and justified norm represents an already trodden path in the knowledge of the truth. Thus it transmits an accumulation of discerned truths to which all reason, open to problems and aiming for "objectivity", must refer if it does not want to fall back on to what is already acquired, or even to see itself lose, should the occasion arise, what would only be accessible in that way. This remains necessary even if reason, in the course of the concrete process of assimilation, penetrates as far as the discovery of knowledge issuing in new solutions of progress.

The more normative reason expressed by a norm or a constellation of norms explains itself directly by the internal logic of its foundations, and this, whether it is a question of complex fundamental relationships or very simple and elementary ones, the more such concomitant exterior criteria lose their importance for the process of its

justification. Thus nobody will have in mind to measure the
reasonable character of a regulation of traffic or of an idea
of defense or a system of social insurance by their age, nor
to make the conviction which one has of justice depend on a
philosophical theorem of the diffusion of justice. At what
point it is indeed hardly essential to discuss the generalized
importance and the currently admitted quantitative aspects,
for the constitution and the justification of norms, perhaps
appears better in certain phenomena of elementary behavior,
independent of history by reason of their structural normative
kernal: necessity has been recognized by all men of all eras.
For example, as in the case of gallantry; they have been put
into practice, without there being any need to justify them
by these criteria, given immediately comprehensible logic
adapted to their requirement.

1.2 *"In their concrete form, elements of social order
are conceived and applied by men for men."*

This thesis presupposes that morality and norms do not
govern us as a blind fate, and that moral norms may be challenged. This signifies nothing other than that we recognize
them as our own functional creations. Morality is an "artificial" product of human reason, conceived and applied by men,
for men. This origin morality shares with all that has been
man-made: with language, which no one will pretend is an immediate product of nature; with the interpretations and
theories on our world and its meaning; and finally, with
technical realizations from flints to computers. It cannot
be a question of denying that all these realizations also
depend on givens, conditions, necessities and natural imperatives, but all are the products of man. All, without excep-

tion are artifacts. This is the meaning of morality.

To recognize moral norms as being the work of man means that they remain submitted to our control, that we cannot be content to respond with obedience before them, but we must answer for them, for their elaboration. It is no longer a question of realizing moral norms, but equally of making morally good norms.

Today, it is no longer permitted for us to ask only: do we act reasonably with respect to the received and given morality and its norms? Do we satisfy these norms? We ask moreover: the norms of our morality, which until today regulated our action and which we considered as undeniably valid, even in the cases where we would no longer respect them, are these norms still reasonable? There are not only good and bad actions, but also good and bad norms, laws, prescriptions, institutions, and good and bad commandments which regulate these actions.

1.3 *"In view of their normative character for moral behavior norms must in principle be without ambiguity (transparent). Insofar as they are transparent, they lose their manipulative character."*

This thesis holds the transparency of norms as the constructive stage of their non-manipulative structure. In reality, each one of us is far from always having pierced distinctly to the bottom of the reasonable character of all the norms by which we let ourselves be governed and guided. The realization of this postulate remains consequently the permanent ethical task of man. This is equally valid for the case of theonomous justification, already inaugurated by St. Thomas, which not only recognises the function of critical

development of natural law by divine law, but also a function
of control exercised by natural law with regard to divine law.
Insofar as the doctrine of natural law affirms that the moral
conscience is essential and natural to man, it permits one to
understand the autonomy of the ethic, so important for St.
Thomas: thanks to the moral conscience which is so natural
to him, man may indeed also judge the goodness and justice of
the commandments which God has given him (cf. Contra Gent.
III, 129). From here one maintains a thought already expressed
by Plato (cf. *Euthyphro*, 10d)--that the moral good is good of
itself and not only because God commands it. Even in God's
presence, man is a moral being, he is not in the situation of
a dog which must blindly follow the commandments of his master
without being able to judge their goodness or their justification: Thomas said in explicit terms: he who abstains from
evil-doing only because God ordered, but not because it is
bad, is not fully free. (Cf. Expos. II epist. ad. Cor. III,
3).[3]

These reflections are completed in the continuation of
our argument by a second movement of thought, which examines
the contingency of goodness and human values and the conditional and relational character of ethical norms, against the theological background.

---

3. L. Oeing-Hanoff, "L'Homme: nature ou histoire? Les
Fondements et critères de normes morales à la lumière de la
tradition philosophique", in F. Henrich (ed.), *Loi Naturelle
et ethique chrétiènne*, Munich, 1970, p. 11-47; 29.

2. *"The legitimization of an obligation by a theonomy
(= divine origin of the norm) does not mean that such categories of human action are fixed as absolute. This remains
true for the norms which govern these actions."*

Here Böckle departs from general fact there is, in the
immanent domain of the experience of man, no point of application, which would be logically absolute. To this corresponds the philosophical conscience of "do not dispose" in
an absolute sense. Insofar as the philosophical conscience
interprets man as creature, theological thought integrates
this philosophical explanation with its reflections. If it
then tries to understand reason as created, it modifies
nothing of the structure of this reason. The philosophical
conscience positively confirms the anthropological hypothesis,
according to which man must not absolve himself, whether as
individual or as a collective. It is in the framework of
this experience of the contingency that he must realize the
concreteness of his freedom. The legitimization of "obligation" by a theonomy, means consequently that there is no
absolutization of a categorical moral behavior, nor of the
norms governing it, but rather that a declaration on the unconditional requirement which concerns the totality of moral
life precisely the denial of all absolutization of the categorical. The adoption of the contingency in the confession
of the believer recognizing himself as a creature, will certainly have consequences for the valid concrete judgments at
the time of the elaboration of norms. These are consequences
which appear just as significant from the point of view of

the anthropological experience of contingency.[4]

    2.1 *"Unconditional interpellation of a free man must be realized in particular contingent acts. The concrete act, purely terrestrial, remains open however, in its intelligibility, in the total sense which human reason gives us. The absolute character of ethical interpellation therefore does not issue from the particular act as such (that is to say, neither its object nor its nature), it can only come from the call which an absolute God addresses to the moral reason of a contingent man."*[5]

According to this thesis, all human action receives the call which is ever-present in itself, of a morally absolute obligation, not of the logic of natural circumstances and historical particulars in which this action is realized and from which its concrete normative structure is constituted, but essentially of the opening of that which acts on this absolute foundation and which alone can solicit in an unconditional way. Inversely, this also means that this absolute dimension of human action does not itself procure a concrete and reasonable character of each action. Even more so, man is returned here to the contingent. In order to make explicit his thesis, Böckle cites an argument of W. Kluxen concerning precisely this problem: "When in his metaphysical advancement, speculative reason seizes man in all domains of his power to be as if

---

    4. F. Böckle, p. 291-292.

    5. Cf. J. Fuchs, "Théologie morale et dogmatique", in *Gregorianum*, 50 (1969), p. 699.

placed in a general order oriented towards God, this knowledge becomes "significant" for action, insofar as the fact of
placing in order appears in human action without doubt more
significant as soon as he is integrated to a general order:
however this integration is not immediately regulatory of
action, since the order thus seized by speculative reason is
not realizable by man, it is not for him a "task to be accomplished".[6]

2.2 *"All ethical norms which concern interhuman behavior*
are based on a judgment of preference. There are so many con-
sidered applications formulated by the following rule of pref-
erence: faced with two concurrent values which are mutually
exclusive, man must examine which of the two must merit the
preference in order to realize it by using the preferred
value.[7] Therefore it is a concrete concern even if this
situation does not always find a verbal expression in hypo-
thetical imperatives."

As Schüller has said, normative statements can only be
unconditionally valid, and without exception insofar as synthetic judgments are concerned, "when they realize a goodness
of which it has been demonstrated that it can never compete
with another more important goodness and thus be more worthy

---

6. W. Kluxen, *L'éthique philosophique de S. Thomas
d'Aquin, Walberger Studien*, Phil. Reihe, Vol. II, Mayence,
1964, p. 62ff.

7. B. Schüller, "Problématique des énoncés éthiques
généraux", in *Theologie und Philosophie*, 45 (1970), p. 3.

of preference".[8] It is possible to design such a goodness
among the "goods". Starting from this fact Böckle establishes,
with Schüller, the rule of preference cited above. Böckle continues, on the concept of hypothetical imperatives:

"They order or defend an action not for itself, but because it--by virtue of a generally reasonable assessment of
'goods'--realizes within the conditions that it is possible
to know, the superior value. Traditional moral theology has
always been conscious of the contingent character of its moral
prescriptions. In the manuals, most of the statements are
classified in the category of conditional morality. Two rules
are the only exceptions in the interpersonal domain: the prohibiting of perjury and the prohibiting of all sexual acts pre-
venting conception. In these two cases, one speaks of absolute
morality, and of absolute intrinsic malice. All the ideological quarrels about the anti-natural character of such acts
the conviction is increasingly widespread today that perjury
and active contraception also carry contingent values, which
must be considered as under the same title as their concurrent
values and that consequently, we are dealing with conditional
morality. In the face of the thomist doctrine of natural law,
this point of view is not strictly speaking a revolutionary
novelty. St. Thomas is indeed convinced that man must, in
thinking reasonably, recognize as good the conservation of the
individual and that of his kind, but that all concrete prescriptions to protect those two 'goods' necessarily embody so
many contingent circumstances, that they simply have no value

---

8. B. Schüller, p. 4.

in themselves, but that they must be considered as generally valid (ut in pluribus)."[9]

2.3 *"The universal value of ethical norms--insofar as they are not purely analytical--signifies more precisely that they are valuable in general, that is to say, that they are valuable insofar as they express the universal, but take into account as much as possible, and in a pertinent manner, circumstances or conditions necessary for concrete action."*

This means that the particular norms need not be given either in the blind absolute or in the arbitrariness of chance, but that they must be seen normally in the context of other concurrent norms, and placed, conforming to the rule of preference, with these in an internal order, of which they receive the degree and the extent of exigency which validates them according to the case.

Thesis 3 now applies this to the confirmation and to the proclamation of norms by the Magisterium. The hypothesis remains: all of the concrete normative statements are not categorical, but hypothetical and contingent statements.

3. *"The confirmation and the proclamation by the Magisterium of hypothetical ethical norms does not abolish their hypothetical character. The confirmation insofar as it does not confer any absolute character on them, that is to say, that norms do not become valid without exception and in all circumstances."*

---

9. F. Böckle, p. 284-285.

174

3.1 *"Revelation does not suppress the logical formal structure of ethical normalcy. The hypothetical character of a prescriptive principle could only be abolished if, by a declaration of the Magisterium, a contingent value became absolute."*

In another place, Böckle states that the determination of possible priorities of certain values over other known values does not abolish the general given, which is the contingency. "This verification appears almost banal; but it means nonetheless that the confirmation and proclamation by the Magisterium, insofar as they do not confer to moral norms any absolute character, that is to say, that the norms do not become valid without exception and in all circumstances. We suppose thus that a possible Revelation modifies the logical formal structure of normalcy as little as does human discourse itself."[10]

3.2 *"Dogmas which, under a descriptive form, express a certain number of truths about God and men, are significs for human action, but they are still not immediately regulators. They are able to become and thus fix a normative contents while arriving at expressing themselves in an evident affirmation on a value."*

What was said in principle, in the citation of W. Kluxen (Thesis 2.1), about the significance of metaphysical statements on man in their importance for human action is affirmed here, by analogy, by the relationship of dependence between the theological declarations of the Revelation on one hand, and human

---

10. F. Böckle, p. 285.

action on the other hand. The truths about God, about Trini-
tarian life, about Incarnation, the Cross, the Resurrection
and the final Accomplishment are not "realizable" by man; the
reality they envisage does not enter into the category of
"tasks to be accomplished". But insofar as man discovers himself as a being concerned in the faith by this reality and
that he recognizes himself as being included in it, it accen-
tuates for him the specific foundation of the interpretation
and the realization of his action. Etiology and eschatology,
theology of the Kairos, theology of the Incarnation, of the
Cross and the Resurrection involve anthropological and theological conceptions of specific action.

4. *"The ethical problem before us which is caused by the
progress of science and technology with their new possibilities of planification, does not consist so much in the use of
means and methods as such, as in the fixing of goals and in
the relationship of the goal to the means."*

In thesis 1 to 3 the priority was given to the question
of the structure of power proper to ethics. Moral norms can
give rise to manipulation.

Thesis 4 now turns to the question of possibilities of
choices of technical means in the process of power of man over
man, possibilities whose variety and range grow with the rise
of modern science. It is still only a question here of this
particular group of means, by which man has begun to influence
in proportions unknown to him before now, on physiological,
economic, psychological and socio-cultural laws which empiri-
cally determine him. Such an enterprise appears absolutely
legitimate in the light of a theological anthropology which,
starting from the project presiding at his creation, under-

stands man as a being responsible for himself and called upon
to transmit a human meaning to reality. However, it must also
be taken into account the fact that all progress in the knowledge of empirical laws which condition the being and the power-
to-be of man, is only possible by increasing specialization
and delimitation and a method of fragmentary observation. But
this precisely is not without its own dangers. We have visibly
arrived at a point where we cannot do more than we are permitted to do, and this is why we are no longer permitted to do
all that we are able. It appears to me totally inadequate, in
spite of everything, to condemn, with Horkheimer and others,
this "instrumental reason" tending towards objectivism and
leading to a method of fragmentary observation. Moreover, it
must remain, everywhere and always, subordinate insofar as
"reason of means" to the real aim, which is the amelioration
of the human condition, and receive thereby moral justice and
dignity. Ethical judgement of technical means and methods
consequently can only issue from the determination of aims
and the corresponding relationship between the goal and the
means.

On this basis, the more precise developments of Thesis 4
in Theses 4.1 and 4.2 appear as complementary determinations
which fix legitimacy and limits on all choice of means in
referring to the general directional value of humanity.

4.1 *"If all ethical norms are considered applications of
the rule of preference, it is no longer possible to speak of
means whose use would be bad in itself, that is to say, inde-
pendently of all possible circumstances. This is valid, in
the traditional domain of eugenics, for surgical sterilization
and artificial insemination (even heterological). In principle*

*it is also valid for the use of new methods (transplantation
of the cellular nucleus or direct influence on genetic information)."*

4.2 *"All technical intervention in the vital process and
in the vital substance of man (anthropotechnical) envisage in
general the amelioration of the human condition in the widest
sense of the word. The respect for the moral person and for
his freedom thus represents a relatively superior value."*

We have thus acquired the general criteria with the help
of which it is possible to morally establish not only the
normative solutions for the normal case—therefore the solutions of a highly concrete general value—but also those which
concern, in extreme situations, the *conflictual case*. Because
here also, it is a question of having access to the solutions
which, in the frame of concrete possibilities, allow realization of that which is better in such a situation. The process
of autodetermination of man, with a view to an amelioration of
the human condition, does not pass by a block condemnation or
a taboo of certain means and measures, but it is by the utilization of the latter which would respect the relationships and
proper conditions in each individual case.

However this does not necessarily prevent one from also
taking into account the secondary effects and the possible
repercussions of each decision of intervention and planning.
This is particularly true for the future possibilities, stated
by Böckle, of directly influencing genetic information. Karl
Rahner has already, and justly, drawn attention to the danger
of irreversibility of certain procedures of intervention in
the domain of anthropotechnics, which could lead to human
situations with no solution. Such a danger can only be

averted insofar as the plan of intervention has in view, aiming for the best, the amelioration of the human condition.[11]

But this implies two things:

On one hand that the plan should live on the simple truth, according to which the object of all planning and all programming is and must remain a *subject*, if the plan is to be realized. This character of the subject, given with the me of man, proves to be inalienable in reality, this, not only in the sense of a "duty", but also, insofar as the social procedures of intervention fundamentally concern persons, consequently beings capable of understanding and approbation, really in the sense of a "being". It follows that a social intervention, which would have as its goal to reduce man to the radical availability of a natural unreasoning object, only capable of reaction, would finally cancel everything, even the very condition of his existence: beings incapable of response, beings incapable of understanding cannot be socially directed.

On the other hand, the plan must be such that furthermore does not require from individuals a blind obedience and performance, as the only possible attitude in the face of his normative demand, but that at the same time it permits them a maximum of responsibility and initiative, this in order to guarantee the character of reason and truth therein. Because, only a program of intervention which authorizes contradiction, which therefore integrates the normative critical reason of individuals into the normative reason of the plan itself, in

---

11. On that which follows, cf. also W. Korff, *Norme et moralité*, p. 164ff.

a permanent process of intentional return to the self, safe-
guards the chances of amelioration with a view to that which
would be better.

4.3 *"The judicious application of the principle of
totality requires that one take into account, not only the
personal and physical dimension, but also the social and al-
truistic dimension."*

We just saw that a systematic elucidation of the empirical laws which condition the being and power-to-be of man,
such as humanities and social sciences attempt, is only possible thanks to objectivism, growing delimitation and specialization and to a method of fragmentary observation. Modern
science essentially exists in the method of *isolation* of
causal relationships as the only method of permitting an
adequate therapy.

It is why Dietrich von Oppen sees, justly, in the utilization of this principle of isolation "an ethical necessity
fundamental to our modern world", without which progress in
the amelioration of the human condition itself would no longer
be conceivable. But on the other hand, he underlines the
dangers connected with a noncritical utilization of this
principle: "To abstract and to isolate means *to eclipse.*
But to eclipse is only separated by one step from *to blind.*
Reality does not let itself decompose in isolated parcels.
It is a fabric of multiple relationships not actually dis-
sociable. The modern conscience, which isolates and constructs in isolated models, courts the danger at every instant of not perceiving it and of letting the necessary

eclipse change in blindness."[12] In order to guard against this possible danger of a practice based solely on this principle of isolation, Böckle has recourse, with reason, to the *principle of totality*, known to reflection in moral theology, in order that it serves as the necessary complement. Böckle however puts forth his reasons as to this principle that, contrary to the traditional understanding, which is so often limited to purely physical integrity, he must refer to a global view of man, that is to say to the whole of physical, personal and social dimensions.[13]

Such a concept of the totality which refers to the global reality of the human condition, makes it clear that all choices of means, as all elaboration of norms governing the choice and utilization of the means, receive from this totality the statute of a contingency, which simultaneously confers on them a rigorous necessity, that is to say, withdraws them from all arbitrary as well as absolute demand.

5. *"In moral theology, the way in which one generally treats the phenomenon of power in the domain of human relationships attaches too little importance to the structural foundations of power in social and economic relationships."*

---

12. D. v. Oppen, "Questions éthiques soulevées par les remèdes modernes", in *Zeitschrift für Theologische Ethik*, 9 (1965), p. 239-247; 241.

13. Cf. F. Böckle, "Aspects éthiques de la transplantation d'organes chez l'homme", in *Studium Generale*, 23 (1970), p. 444-459; 451ff.

In this and in the following theses, the fundamental
ethical problem of power of man over man unveiled up to this
point, now poses the question about the effective structures
of the power, at the concrete sociological level. If this is
only expressed here by a few allusions, the indication furnished by Böckle does appear to me extremely important: even
a morally legitimate power, researching the human as the final
value, is never exercised in a space exempt from all power.
The theological reflections on the acquisition and the exercise of power usually start from the postulate that power in
the hand of man must in itself be appreciated in a positive
fashion. In accordance with this "classical" definition of
Max Weber, power is considered then as an opportunity of im-
posing one's will within a group of social relationships, in
spite of the resistance manifest there. Power, as opportunity, is thus above all understood as a possibility possessed
by a person and a group of persons respectively. It is evident that theology also knows the dangers connected to an
opportunity of this kind, each time that one uses it for
erroneous ends, that is to say, ends that are egotistical
and for the exclusive profit of the group. It is precisely
because it knows it, that it requires from the one who bears
the social responsibility that he can renounce neither the
seizure of the possession, nor the exercise of power, which
permits him to oppose an unjust exercise of this power and
to thus provoke a more just equilibrium. Justice examined
under different aspects thus becomes the measure which authorizes judgment of the distribution and the exercise of power.[14]

14. Th. McMahon, "The Moral Aspects of Power", *Concilium*,
90 (1973), p. 51-65.

There is a place to treat a double objection of the phenomenon of power in this way:

1. If, remaining entirely or neutral in preference, one only perceives in power a given opportunity, one is logically led to neglect the fact, that all power is established in very precise social conditions. Even if one refuses to admit in a unilateral fashion that the relationships of productions (capital-work), according to the marxist theory, are the background which determine all the relationships, it is necessary, however, to consider it certain that the previous conditions of the battle and of the defense of interests are to be, for certain groups in our society, the most unequal. The prevailing conditions of this kind thus give occasion to the manifest inequality of opportunities. The analysis and the criticism of these conditions should, in a treatise of moral theology which would take the real into account, occupy the first place.

2. It is necessary to say again, that it follows immediately that theology cannot undertake this critical analysis without assistance. The respect due to established powers--aside from the case of an evidently tyrannical regime--has always been a constant, in the doctrine of the Church. The relationships of force, effectively established, enjoy, so to speak, the presumption of the right of continuity. This presupposition would be, in each case, to submit to a critical text, failing which the criterion of justice applied to the exercise of power appears a priori under an unfavorable light.

Humanization of human power necessarily includes the humanization of family, political, social and economic structures.

But what are, from the point of view of empirical sociology, the real instigators and agents of the change of struc-

tures? It is to this question that Böckle tries to respond
in his last thesis.

6. *"The most recent experiences on conformity will show
that it is not really the majority which exercises a power
over the individual but that a unified and coherent minority
may influence the general norm."*

Böckle refers here to a report of Jos Jaspars, "The Power
of the Majority".[15] According to him, one may admit as experimentally proven that, in groups, similar directions, agreements and conformities in the normative conscience exist essentially through the resolute influence of unified and organized minorities. "The operative factor in the influencing
process is the *consistency* shown by the majority."[16] The
truth of this is evident, not only for the validity of norms,
which are decreed by a majority of political and moral author-
ities, considered as a "governing minority", but also for the
validity of normative innovations "coming from below", which
go along with the state of effective conscience of the majority and coincide with it, on the condition, however, that these
innovations be defended by a coherent minority, with conviction and constancy. "Conformism is only one of the forms in
which social influence is exercised. Innovation, whereby
current ideas and norms upheld by the majority are altered
at the instance of a minority is the (hopeful) reverse side
of the coin, which up to now has hardly been looked at."[17]

15. J. Jaspars, *Concilium*, 90 (1973), p. 19-27.

16. Jaspars, p. 26.

17. Jaspars, p. 27.

184

CONTRIBUTION OF PROFESSOR SCHÜLLER
OF THE UNIVERSITY OF BOCHUM,
ON THE SUBJECT OF THESIS 2.2
OF PROFESSOR BÖCKLE

I am not entirely satisfied with the citation of Mr. Böckle here, which is extracted from an article[1] where I tried for the first time to present the problem: the first attempts at formulating a problem are rarely satisfactory.

I will allow myself to outline the problem which Mr. Böckle treats in his lecture and which I see in the following manner. We find in Catholic moral theology but also in Protestant theology, among other things, two types of norms for action: I am only concerned here with norms for action and I will not discuss norms of intention.

The first type of norm has preoccupied us particularly in our debates about contraception: "You must not make use of any contraceptives whatever may be the consequences"--The use of contraceptive measures is therefore never permitted, even if it became the only possible way to avoid the catastrophe which would be caused by over-population. Another classic example of this type of norm is the forbidding of lying, for example, as Kant and Fichte conceive it, "You cannot lie, even if it is the only possible way to save an innocent man." In Anglo-American vocabulary, norms of this kind are sometimes called "moral absolutes", or deontological.

1. Br. Schüller, "Problématique des énoncés éthiques généraux", in *Theologie und Philosophie*, 45 (1970), p. 3.

Here is the question: Is there any evidence for the basis of these deontological norms? I believe I can furnish the proof that the justifications given by Catholic tradition are inconsistencies.

A first inconsistency is in the ethical judgment brought to contraception: it consists, in brief, of declaring that the (natural) preestablished finalities of certain organs and certain functions of man are intangible.

The other inconsistency is in the norms bearing on that which tradition calls "the intrinsically bad acts by default of law in the person who acts....This inconsistancy consists with reference to the exclusive sovereign powers of God, in refusing to accord to man certain full powers, as if there exists between God and man concurrent relationships. A few examples: Man must not kill himself, because only God is master of life and death; because he unites in marriage man and woman, God only might eventually separate them again. In brief, the tradition is incapable of bringing to the deonto-logical norms which it claims to impose, the basis which with-stands all tests.

It is true that tradition knows another way of establish-ing norms. One has taken the habit of calling this type of norm telcological. Americans and English also speak of "con-sequentialism". In this sense, moreover, an act is always judged morally by the consequences which it involves. Then the problem comes back to procurring criteria which would per-mit the appraisal of the consequences of an action. The great danger consists in proceeding with naïvete, with which one re-proaches J. Fletcher with good reason. Understood in this sense, the supreme rule of preference, as I have given it, and as Mr. Böckle has cited it, becomes unintelligible. From this rule one cannot for example, without other diversified rules, making use of mediations, take a position on artificial insemination.

The task which is incumbent upon us today, upon us, the moral theologians, seems to me to be, after all has been said, the following: How can we convey the ways of action, which up to today tradition has established as deontological norms, as plausible teleological justifications?

PART TWO

Perspectives of Research

GROUP I

(French Speaking Scholars)

Responsibility as to the Quality of Life

Before considering responsibility, it is necessary to see
clearly the meaning of "quality of life".

1. What is understood by "quality of life"?

This idea seems to appear implicitly in societies of cultures where one succeeds in satisfying principal primary needs,
where it becomes possible to go beyond the concern for survival
and reach that for better living. This may manifest itself,
for example, in the research of an art of living or of greater
comfort, or in that of the elimination of constraints; this
may lead, for example, to a restriction of births in order to
favor the social ascension of the following generation.

The fact that this varies according to the culture and
even according to the individual shows that it is a more subjective idea, and therefore affected by a certain coefficient
of relativity.

One talks explicitly of the quality of life since the recent industrialization has given wealthy countries a general
liberty with respect to the primary needs, and at the same
time has secreted threats against the quality of life attained
in this manner: it is the natural human environment that one
feels is endangered by overcrowding, pollution, the repression
of natural resources. These threats engendered by progress
now reach basic elements like air or water which have not been
in danger until now. The weight of industrial society equally

makes us discover the vital necessity of protecting the possibilities of man's moral and cultural blossoming.

If one wants to give a foundation for the quality of life, to defend it or promote it, one is led to research the general principles which situate it in a scale of values, and therefore in a total conception of man. Revelation guides and animates Christians in this search. The declarations of the rights of man are located in this quest.

2. Responsibility of man:

This reference to superior principles proves to be so much more necessary as the pluralism of cultures or of social classes leads to a concurrence between the qualities of life of the different groups which coexist within the same entity: building, city, nation, or world. It would not be necessary, to assure quality of life, for a group or individual to suppress or diminish that of another, by war, racism, economical exploitation or diverse injustices. Nor is it necessary to forget to take into account the future generations; this confronts us with demographic responsibility.

GROUP II

(French Speaking Scholars)

*Faith and Morality with Respect to
the Powers of Man over Himself*

Our group decided to focus its reflection on a precise
problem: the experiments of human fecondation in vitro.

We began by situating them in the general perspective of
the moral situation of our time. The static view of a World
ordained to preserve and the individualist Ethic which springs
from it give place to *the dynamic conception* of a cosmos becoming humanized. Humanity is tested in a new way: conquering, creative and responsible for its destiny. Confronted with
the unprecedented problems issuing from its multiform praxis,
it must exercise with respect to them a constantly recurring
critical judgment. Ethics, without ceasing to be personalist,
acquires a historical, social and collective dimension.

Faith, as such, does not furnish Christians with ready-
made answers nor with obvious facts in the face of the questions posed by science, technology and life. Nevertheless,
the certainty that God the creator, who entrusted the world
to man, continues to convey through the work of men, toward
the end inaugurated by the Resurrection of Jesus, the active
presence, at the heart of the Christian and within the People
of God, of the very mind of Jesus, must have some influence on
judgment as well as on action. Working with other men for the
completion of the world and embarked with them on a communal
adventure, of which Faith knows the significance, Christians
have to be attentive to what happens in order to discern its

meaning and to orient it toward the Truth. This prudent, and communal discernment, held in dialogue, does not go without rational, precise and competent analysis, which certainly does not always lead to compelling and unanimous answers in matters so complex and relative. Nor does it accept the sacrifice of technical commitment and fascination of knowledge to the criteria of efficiency.

In approaching the precise problem which we would set before ourselves in this perspective, we question ourselves.

1) The desire of man today is to master his fertility as totally as possible, with a view to decisively ameliorating the human condition. Is this desire legitimate? We are unanimous in answering "yes".

2) If experimentation is the indispensable necessity of scientists, does it make all experiments legitimate, including those of fecundation in vitro?

A voice is raised to affirm that the only legitimate fertilization is that which results from a normal sexual encounter.

Others assert that it is legitimate to make *all* kinds of experiments: They feel particularly uneasy about the inevitable "sacrifice" of fertile eggs. Is this not a criminal attempt on a human being, which is as malicious as abortion?

Others finally admit that there is a radical difference between refusing to let an embryo grow in its natural conditions for development and the acceptance of the death of a laboratory blastula. They emphasized the decisive importance of these experiments for the future of humanity; the doubt which hovers over the human status of the fertilized egg, doubt which neither Revelation, nor Tradition, nor Science is in the condition to remove; the irreparable imperfection and

the inherent tentativeness in experimental research, and conclude positively in favor of experimentation as we know it
today.

As they say that they are incapable, as theologians, of
deciding in an absolute fashion, we appeal in confidence to
the consciences of Christian scholars, not without leaving
the question open. Because one would not know how to treat
biological animal material and human elements in exactly the
same way.

GROUP III

(German Speaking Scholars)

*The Role of Faith in Resolving
the Moral Problem of the Power of Man over Man*

The problem is stated in the question: in what sense and to what extent does the Christian faith find essential norms in morality? The group established this fact: statements of faith are by their very structure descriptive statements whereas ethical statements have an imperative character. Faith immediately involves a statement on existence, even concerning what is unique and personal. On the contrary, the ethical statement immediately involves a question. In spite of this, the statement of faith has its importance in the realm of ethics. Indeed it does not announce statements which would only concern that which God does for man's salvation, but it also establishes the first elements of theological anthropology. There, after the manner of a preliminary anthropological decision, one discerns an expanse of meaning and interpretation which directly or indirectly, admits at least ethical conclusions situated on the logical slope of meaning. For example, this is also true for the concept of personality which is raised in our subject: "Man faced with a God who transcends history", allows the revelation of a unique comprehension of the human personality: norms of morality are put into service for the perfect security of a human existence which will not be repeated. The eschatological justification frees man and all human judgement which would be absolute and definitive (the question of capital punishment). The doctrine of a

personal survival after death of the body creates an ultimate
freedom of man with respect to social structures: indeed, the
person is not a function of a society which one would imagine
to be absolute. This preliminary decision of the anthropological type procures a framework of values, in the interior
of which the concrete norms of morality are put to work. In
this respect one has established that to make up one's mind
concretely in favor of a given anthropology, is already a
decision of morality: it does not belong to the domain of
everyone's capacity for free decision. The truth of this preliminary decision of the anthropological type must indeed furnish its proof in dialogue and criticism. This being done,
the decisive criterion can only be in a vaster realization of
human existence. This criterion is not fixed a priori; on the
contrary one acquires it by the understanding of history associated with experience. Moreover, it may well be that the
Christian and the non-Christian are in accord in supporting
a concrete judgment of morality, however it remains to be
known, whether this accord goes as far as the foundations,
and whether one cannot imagine situations in which Christians
and non-Christians oppose each other in their concrete judgment. It is advisable to take into account that in the context of a Christian anthropology, irreversable affirmations
command recognition.

GROUP IV

(French Speaking Scholars)

Experience and Norms:
The Mediating Role of the Moralist

1) Moral norms are called upon to express a certain
wisdom of human action in an epoch and in a culture.

Whence did these norms originate? Experience according
to us, plays an irreplaceable role here.

Only actual and considered experiences progressively
allow for norms to be elaborated and received, through a
rather large consensus.

We see here a primary role of the moralist: aiding to
disclose the valid and general nature of experience, which is
always lived as unique and original, and to express it in
formulae which may render it enlightening and normative for
the whole.

2) However, constantly and particularly in our epoch of
rapid change, certain norms are no longer received by an important part of the people. It happens that many refuse these
norms not so much for the reason of difficulties which they
might find in practicing them, but because they do not appear
to express to them a truth of human action, which they consider closer to their new behavior.

Thus, it appears to be important that those who can no
longer accept the coherence of acquired norms, for reason of
their contradiction in their estimation with respect to their
interior requirements, are not, by virtue of this fact, secondary. It is for the moralist to welcome the validity of

this dispute, which may result in some new coherence. Change and progress are not possible without the contribution and the acceptance of experiences partly divergent with respect to the recognized moral order.

Moreover, breaks provoked by the multiplicity and the acceleration of cultural change, and similarly by the intimate mixture of diverse cultures, lead us to think that a certain ethical pluralism must find its place today, and even be imposed.

All this requires the effort of listening, confrontation and discernment which also constitutes the task of the moralist.

3) Consequently, the moralist is led to ask himself the question about the criteria of discernment.

For this subject, it is important to make two preliminary remarks: on one hand, this discernment is not only, nor primarily, the task of moralists. It is at the concrete level and at that of the confrontation of diverse experiences which, above all, discernment develops.

On the other hand, one must allow life to develop, without wishing to prematurely circumscribe it within norms. No exterior criterion can ever replace the wisdom of actual experience.

The research into elements of discernment for the moralist has only been outlined. Among these criteria, it seems necessary to be attentive:

---to a certain coherence of action finding its expression in an internal logic of different aspects,

---to the consensus progressively resulting from different individual experiences,

---to the regard for fidelity to all the aspects of an experience in order to safeguard its global character,

---to seek out dialogue with other different or complementary experiences,

---etc.....

4) Are the conditions of moral elaboration, and therefore the role of experience, fundamentally modified when they concern the Christian life?

It seems not to us.

Christianity contributes an illumination which is fundamentally new in the orientation of existence, in the discovery of the only Law which is that of the love of God present at the heart of human history. There is no behavior which is necessarily bound to this primordial discovery. This may be interpreted in ethics, differentiating according to the cultures and human groups.

Consequently it is incumbent upon the moralist to contribute to the prevention of the improper establishment of ethical norms in an absolute which is indissociable from the Christian faith. This is just as much necessary to allow access to new moral coherences as not to engulf the faith in contingent options.

In our capacity as moral theologians, it is for us to pursue with everyone this work of mediation between experience and norms, in the line of interpretation of the Gospel.

(French Speaking Scholars)

Humanization of Man:
The Psychoanalytic Approach

From a group comprising psychoanalysts and moral theologians, from the latter come some statements and questions.

Ethics seems to offer the humanization of man (personal level-social level). What can psychoanalysis contribute to this proposition?

1) Importance of the law, of the norm.

It is only in interiorizing a certain number of norms and interdicts (the forbidding of incest, etc....) that man starts on the way to the truth of his desire.

If desire is a condition of the law, the law itself is a condition of the validity of desire.

More globally, man is born into a previously existing world, structured by language. If the authority of the Church makes this primordial structure and its history appear and be known, if it also allows a stance of liberating distance, it would not deny the necessity for a milieu structured by norms as a condition for human life, that is to say, a relational life.

However, the necessary existence of norms is one thing, but the content of those norms is another.

2) Norms and narcissism.

When the moralist, the confessor, the pastoral counselor, recall the existence of a concrete norm "to respect", what do they do? Are they not moved by the desire that their inter-

locutor should return to them a satisfactory image of themselves? Is this not narcissism which should be denounced; a
narcissism which intends to make the other nothing but an
image of oneself?

But when the same people return the interlocutor to his
own informed freedom, are they not moved by the desire that
the latter should respond to an image of themselves to be
otherwise and free? One does not avoid narcissism. It is
therefore necessary to distinguish a narcissism which wants
to alienate the other from oneself and a narcissism which
wants the other to be simultaneously alike and different.
One function of moral discourse seems to be to reinstate the
first form of narcissism.

3) Man as a relational being.

At the heart of the analytic approach is the experience
of interpersonal relationships. If the word "moral" is
avoided, a great many properly ethical words come into psy-
choanalytical language. One will discover the conditions of
a "valid" intersubjectivity: the surrendering of man to his
desire (this "gaping void"), yielding to a "need".

It is this desire and this need of the other which are
the conditions of a true relationship, insofar as they cause
the appearance of and promote the encounter between simili-
tude and difference.

Finally, a certain number of interdicts and fundamental
norms must play a part in the analytical relationship: to
break the relationship of dependence (love of money), to keep
the "benevolent neutrality", refusing to counsel or to aid,
the norm of being simply oneself and other in order to allow
the other to become himself....

In conclusion, as all human sciences, psychoanalysis has a simultaneously partial and total projection (perspective on the totality of man). There remains in question the problem of its articulation with the other human sciences and therefore the problem of multidisciplinary research in view of this humanization of man.

GROUP VI
(German Speaking Scholars)
*Biological Determinism and Ethical Normalcy
in Human Behavior*

I. BIOLOGICAL DETERMINISM

1. *Statement of the problem*

The theme chosen for our reflection implicitly raises the
question of the autonomy of man in the following manner: effectively, are there laws of life which mark it in advance and
determine human behavior? The concept of biological determinism remains problematic: the group proposed to use the word
"programming". What does this word mean? On one hand, it is
indispensable to see man as a living being: the Aristotelian
definition of "zoon legon echon" adds an accent on language
and reason. On the other hand, however, man passes beyond the
structure of the living. Therefore agreements and differences
exist in the interior of the concept of a living being and it
is not possible to reduce man to a biological programming.

2. *Analogically moral behavior--details about this concept
in behavioral research*

If one identifies perfectly the morality and the specific
freedom of man, there cannot be analogically moral behavior in
an animal. However, on the contrary, if one really wishes to
disclose the so-called material object (= the contents) of
the morality in the behavior of living beings, and to save

the formal object of morality for human beings, one may de-
limit the meaning of the word "analogy": on the one hand,
it is necessary to understand it from the point of view of
behavioral psychology, on the other hand, not to press this
philosophical concept too hard and content oneself with seeing in it a way of marking that which is homologous. Here
the analogy expresses that which is similar in spite of a
different origin. The homologous, on the contrary, comprises the dependence on the origin (commentary made on the
lecture of Mr. Illies, no. 5).

3. *The importance of biological programming for ethics*

Do the criteria exist which permit modification of biological programming? What are their limits, in order that a
modification does not imply destructive sequels? Would biological programming be a return to the ethic of existence?
What does one think of St. Thomas Aquinas' sentence: "Animals
are given to us as examples"?

Thus the discussion begins.

II. ETHICAL NORMALCY

In this discussion, one will try to give precise details
about the position set forth by a conference member, Mr. Rombach; to seize on its point of departure in a critical way, in
short to predict the repercussions in the domain of normalcy
in predominantly theological ethics. The keen interest manifested by the participants is explained by the fact that the
mediation of anthropology between theology and the human sci-

ences seemed to Mr. Rombach to be the indispensable condition
for elaboration of ethical norms.

1. *Basic principle*

Different questions about the place to be accorded to
new concepts--experimentation, model, game--and to the importance of the experience of autonomy for the normative ethic,
led Mr. Rombach to develop the following thought:

a) In the course of the process of the quest and experience of the self a "structural genesis" of ethics ("Struk-
turgenese") is constituted. During this process, the faculties of a man develop, each assuming a corrective role with
respect to the others. When all the possibilities are ex-
hausted, the process reaches the stage of "success" ("Gelung-
enheit"). Success in this case means legalization, normalcy.
This normalcy is therefore not imposed from the exterior, it
comes from the interior. Consequently, it is born experimentally from the structural genesis.

b) Normalcy arising in the course of the process of the
quest of the self is "new". Here, this novelty is not a
synonym of a total abolition of a preceding normative system,
but rather a new structuring. One might call it "translation"
("Verschiebung"). For example: translation of a daily and
habitual linguistical system into poetic language. The words
remain the same, their meaning changes in the new context.
It is in this sense that there is modification in each process
of the quest of the self, whether it involves an individual or
a group.

c) Normalcies coming from the structural genesis are
plural. Their plurality is superior to the number of individuals. Today a plurality of structures of the ethos

exists, between which one establishes, if one researches
the common ethical foundation, the existence of connections
which only translation and interpretation may render accessible. Moreover here the ethical structures correct each
other. Thus is realized, in the praxis of the group and of
the individual, the unity between the diverse structures of
the ethos. One passes from one structure to another. This
is why the most important requirement of an ethical structural genesis, as much on the theoretical level as on the
practical level, is the exercise of translation.

2. *"Concreativity"--grace and human realization*

Question: one of the distinctive traits of ethical structural genesis is "concreativity" ("Konkreativität"). It is
differentiated from the act of fabrication (= artificial) in
that it sees "success" not only as its own product, but also
as a "grace". Do we in this case have to contend with a
plurality of realizations by grace of success, and no longer
with a concrete normative world?

Mr. Rombach calls these plural realizations "models", and
cites as example the model of "poverty" of St. Francis of
Assisi. In assuming it, and therefore recreating it as *his*
form of life, St. Francis confers a universal value on this
model. Models are comparable to ethical "fundamental words",
susceptible to being translated by each other (e.g. the virtues).

All the domains of existence are certainly not submitted
to the process of concreativity. Structural genesis has always led to systems of behavior which we believe to be given
normalcies (e.g. the regulation of traffic). The systems are
the later forms of created models. They also find their place

in the new creative research of norms, but this time the
priority of the system such as it is known to the ethics of
"former times", must yield to the priority of the model.

3. *Question: is "concreativity" a philosophical or theological category?*

Is "grace" in the ethical structural genesis a structural
element of the philosophical order--a positive formulation of
this moment of non-availability in the quest for the human
self--or rather a category of a priori existential religion?

Mr. Rombach pleads in favor of the identity of theological and philosophical aspects and, according to him, the theological categories are modified, not from the exterior, but
by inner experience. They are accessible to everyone's experience, and the very fact that they are fundamentally accessible to experience proceeds from the principle of the Incarnation belonging to Christianity. From this, one can say
that Christianity has the only "realistic" anthropology.

The idea of "grace" must be reinterpreted from "concreativity". It would be necessary then to analyse the manner in
which it is transmitted by social ties (interpersonal level)
and simultaneously to determine its relationship with the freedom of man (by reason of the History of Creation and of Salvation).

4. *Biological programming--"indeterminate nature" ("unvorge-
pragt")--experimental birth of human nature*

Question: if the nature of man is born in the course of
ethical structural genesis in a quasi-experimental way, does
no previous given exist; does each one begin "ab ovo"? What
then is the meaning of accumulated experience and historical

tradition? Is there not a naturally determined part of the nature of man, at least in the line of reflections above about biological programming?

Mr. Rombach considers human nature as "indeterminate" insofar as it is particularly *human* nature (all predetermination must be understood as specifically pre-human). Considering structural genesis at the individual level, one is led to say that the "person" is born progressively. It is not a fixed given, realized by the sequel, but the "success", which is only the final end of the process. The Christian concept of "person" can only be conserved at the price of such a reinterpretation. This is equally valid for the concept of society.

History is characterized by the fact that the interval between the upheavals grows smaller. This interval has become so short that upheavals are produced in everyone's lives. This explains the disappearance of this stability engendered by the equilibrium of an epoch. Man could see in this stability a given "ordo" with which he identified himself. The brief interval between changes today confers a fluctuating character on everything, which obliges man to constantly reinterpret (cf. above: the translation from one structure to another). Nowadays, man is only man insofar as he is reinterpreting himself, and consequently also renewing himself.

The problem of the relationships of this thesis with situation ethics can only be initiated.

5. *Existential misery of man: success and failure*

Question: would one not put too much confidence in the ethical structural genesis? Does not experience itself prove that failure is more widespread than success? Is it not necessary to take seriously the misery of man and his risk of never discovering himself?

Mr. Rombach emphasizes that "misery" is precisely an element indispensable to the structural genesis. According to him, ethical virtues are born from distress. The danger of a minimization of the negativity would disappear, if one makes this the point of departure in the process of the quest for the self (cf..above no. 3). The misery of human existence must not be dissimulated by expedients, psychoanalysis having shown that that is the origin of neurosis. Moreover, negativity must be actual and integrated as that which conditions the possibility of success (e.g. the existentialist interpretation of death). A depreciation of the negativity proceeds from social situations where this negativity seems to be repressed (e.g. the affluent society). The very absence of all negativity is felt as the worst negativity (e.g. revolt of the young generation). This is why negativity is being researched openly in order that it serve as foundation for the new realizations of success. In a Christian point of view, one must take into account the fact that the conversion of the negativity into positivity is a constitutive element of the Christian faith.

6. *Creativity and normalcy*

Question: one objected that Mr. Rombach's thesis seems to reverse the relationship of cause to effect with normalcy and creativity. Normalcy would then be visualized as the secondary system and creativity as the primary event ("structure"). It should be observed that this conception reverses, moreover, the relationship of cause to effect with "synthesis" and "structure", such as it is understood by the theory of systems and structuralism: structures are not relationships within the system, but systems viewed from the genetical angle. The transformation is, from all evidence, considered as a condition of existence and not vice-versa.

The ethics of values and certain interpretations of St. Thomas attempt, each in its own way, this reversal of the relationship of cause to effect. The ethics of values distinguishes between hierarchy of values and the intensity of values. These are specifically human superior values which have the most attenuated restraining character. One must keep oneself from quantitatively interpreting this reversal of the relationship of cause to effect. From the quantitative point of view, normative systems and man's adaptation to them prevail, an adaptation which is felt as a factor of mitigation. From this quantitative point of view, creativity is a particular case of normalcy. This explains the scorn of Tradition which consists in seeing creativity as a borderline case of adaptation to the norm (e.g. *epikie* in post and neoscholasticism). However, for whatever starts from the relationships of cause and effect: structure-system, transformation-stagnation, normalcy is a particular case of creativity. All presently existing normalcies are born of processes and creative models.

With St. Thomas, already, the understanding of normalcy comes from creativity. The Thomist conception of "lex nova" and of "epikie" reverses the relationship of cause to effect, and in doing so, coincides with the Christian conception of law and freedom. Normalcy, in the Christian sense of the word, must above all be understood as a creation, insofar as it is based on the autonomy of man.

7. *Criteria of success and failure*

The problem of the criteria of the ethical structural genesis made difficulties appear in the comprehension of the working group.

In response to diverse questions, Mr. Rombach put forward the idea that one cannot look for other criteria more general than success ("ça va"), this is the most general criterion (norm of norms). This is why one had to develop an internal criteriology for success. The discussion produced the following ideas: logic in the realization of each individuality; acceptance of the consequences proceeding from the concrete choice of values (exclusion of concurrent values); coherence of a corresponding normative system; absence of internal contradictions in the ethical model; validity of the Kantian requirement according to which it is necessary (*muss*) that that which goes (*soll*) for me must go for everyone. Each order succeeds insofar as it reaches the highest degree of structural development which must represent it. A dogmatic fixation of the criteria is excluded by this fact. They are deduced from the intention of the process itself. The "norma normans", success (or "ça va") claims to be the human criterion par excellence, because it assumes the active and creative form of that which is human.

Although a single criteriology outside success does not exist, the role of the moralist consists above all in leading the individual or the group to fully assume the principle of self-creation. Man is not morally determined or programmed, but liberated for his moral self-realization. This is not without its consequences for a pedagogical ethic. Ethics become in and of themselves eminently pedagogical since the critical aid which they contribute may cooperate with the blooming of the structures of the individual ethos (maieutics).

The criteriology of failure appears more embarrassing than the criteriology of success. The human possibilities of fabrication and manipulation seem to permit realization of things which, from an anthropological point of view, can only be considered as a "failure". How to convert them into the "useful"? According to Mr. Rombach, it is here that the need of a scientifically founded ethical criteriology is felt. In our time, the individual is no longer in the process of responding to general demands. There, moral science may serve and aid to reunite the totality of givens, theories and models. However it cannot be a question of prescribing a moral system (N.B. "moral system" not in the sense of the historical moral systems of morality), but to conceive of normalcy capable of being lived. Rombach illustrates the danger of changing the nature which runs through the moral systems born nevertheless from creative structures of ethos, by the example of the history of orders.

With numerous participants, the question of criteria will certainly leave many unsolved problems which only the concrete application to the questions of detail would have been able to explain.

8. *What is the subject of a creative normalcy?*

Question: is an already existing normalcy the condition of the possibility of a creative normalcy? In this case, what role does the social context play? For a model like that of St. Francis, should one not ignore social and normative conditions? Who is the bearer of the ethical structural genesis insofar as the realization of its success is concerned? The individual or a closed society?

For Mr. Rombach, the bearer is the group, although one must not understand it as totally distinct from the individual, nor as a pure and simple accumulation of the processes of the quest for the self. The genetical structures of these ethical processes are, on the contrary, overlapped with each other, they condition and correct each other. Self-creation of the group includes self-creation of the individual and vice-versa (e.g. conjugal life, discussion group, parish). Creation includes the processes of dissolution and constraint at the same time. For example: to experience chaotic traffic presents a double aspect, antimoral and promoral, insofar as the normalcy of traffic would be established at a superior level. From all evidence, this creative normalcy can have no other subject than the free adult man (cf. above no. 6), and, in Christian words, the saved man (cf. Gal. 4). Would this structural ethic not be an ethic of the elite, promoted by certain groups and "imposed" on others? According to Mr. Rombach, creativity is constituted from *all* experience of the self and the group insofar as it is not masked by fixations of systems (e.g. exaggerated fixation to authority). Therefore, the creative normalcy will be, in principle, possible anywhere, with account taken of the restrictions brought in no. 6. If not, the Christian ethic would be no longer possible anywhere, in principle.

9. *Structural ethics and theory of systems*

This structural ethical analysis makes use of the theory of systems (developed above all by linguistics and the social sciences), all the while modifying the context of the meaning.

This is why the words: structure, model, and function must
be understood differently. Rombach refers to it for the historical deduction and the differentiation between structured
thought and the theory of systems of Pascal and Leibnitz.[1]
Beyond the creative and genetic aspects, the particular form
of communication plays a decisive role in structural ethics.
The communication among systems ("intersystemisch") of different ethical structural geneses constitutes a "metaethic" in
this sense, which will thus effectively develop a method of
communication among worlds. It makes parallels appear each
time that it attempts translations. Passing by diverse ethical structures is accompanied by their mutual correction and
in this way, by an amelioration of each of the structures of
ethos. In such a "metaethic", it would be a question of the
ethos of all possible moralities, of the morality of moralities.

10. *Resumé*

The discussion of the position presented by Mr. Rombach
revealed many centers of interest: intellectual curiosity
first desiring to comprehend this position with all its implications (above all the role of concreativity), critical
reflection as to the pertinence and its field of extention,
research of the possibilities of application to the constitution of norms. In spite of the real progress of the discussion, one could not, without being injurious to the questions
themselves, declare them already resolved. The result of the

1. Cf. H. Rombach, *Substanz, System, Struktur.* 2 vols.,
(Freiburg, K. Alber, 1965-1966), for historical information.

common reflections may be foreseen in the fact that the numerous problems of fundamental moral theology were treated and elaborated. The desire appeared to see ethics founded on anthropology in order to face the discoveries of the human sciences on the existent and fabricated programmings (cf. the lecture on 'functioning of manipulation').

III. ASPECTS OF MORAL THEOLOGY

Starting with the theses of M. F. Böckle, the discussion only added a few details:

1) In order to differentiate this particular form of the power of man over man which is the moral norm itself (cf. thesis 1) one proposed another word: for example, "regulation".

2) The thesis of fundamental non-ambiguity and rationality of norms (cf. 1.2 and 1.3) must not be interpreted in a "rationalist" fashion. In a global view, it will require cognitive and affective stages, a rational coherence and an experience of value and of faith.

3) The thesis of the "theonomous legitimization" (cf. 2) raised the question of knowing that which is specifically Christian, to which one could not precisely respond in the sense of a heteronomous power (cf. 2.1: "signifier" but not of immediate use in the regulation of action; cf. also 3.2). The particular place to accord to christological and eschatological aspects might be better developed with the aid of these theses:

4) The "rule of preference" (cf. 2.2 and 4.1) must not be understood here in the pure technological sense; the rule

assumes reflection on the values themselves, their level and their relationship.

5) The "hypothetical character" of norms (cf. 2.2 and 3) does not mean that they have a non-obligatory character, rather that their elaboration is conditioned.

6) According to the participants, the problem of "malo ex objecto" should be made more precise. The discussion showed so many particular aspects that the proposal was made to devote a conference to this theme.

7) *Summary*

Given the subject that was chosen, the working group kept to the themes treated by the lecturers. Unfortunately all of them could not be considered, since a basic text determined the development of these sessions. For this reason, it would be good to see a complement to the lectures in these reflections. Their ternary analysis (biology, anthropology, morality) appeared fully justified, from the methodological point of view. One must, consequently, pay less attention to the insufficiencies of the discussion--the insufficient definition of concrete ethical norms--than to try to see in it a contribution to the research of a method able to lead to the elaboration of concrete ethical norms.

GROUP VII

(French Speaking Scholars)

*The Function and the Diffusion
of Moral Teaching to the People*

The theme which was proposed to our group was the following: the diffusion and the function of moral teaching to the
people. We have taken it up from a viewpoint which I would
define as the research of requirements which are presented to
us by the fact that our theological work is a work for the
Christian communities.

I will divide my account into four points.

1) Reflection is confronted in a permanent way with the
fundamental question of the relationship of theory to praxis.
We vacillated between two representations of this relationship: one emphasizes the presentation, guaranteed by an authority, of a coherent doctrinal whole which is not absolute
and evolutive, coming from the Gospel and from the Christian
tradition; the other takes its point of departure in the life
of persons and communities, with the exercise of a communal
discernment. The criteria of this discernment not being absolute values, but the operating models based on the Gospel and
on Christian Tradition, which are verified and criticized in
experience. We hope that the study of this relationship of
theory to praxis is accentuated in the fundamental research.

2) The possibility of this study is bound to conditions
among which we believe to be able to state the following:
a) that the pluralism of political, economic and cultural

situations is effectively taken into consideration. The existence of an ideological pluralism in our societies appears moreover to require a new definition of competence of their extent, and of their relationships; b) that research is done on all levels in conjunction with the human sciences; c) that this place of research is the competent community, confronted with given historical situations and where the different charismas are exercised in complementarity. (We have asked a question about this: does not the situation of the theologian still appear as a mandarinate?)

3) We have taken note of the criticism of normative discourse of ethics, which has been made several times here. We use another language, characterized by the proposition and the description of Christian existence, an existence which is characterized by the manifestation of the fruits of the Spirit. It appears indispensable to add that moral discourse of the Church must be credible, that is to say, that it must be accompanied by guarantees in acts and in attitudes, on the personal level and also on the institutional level.

4) Whatever may be the orientations of fundamental research, our propositions cannot ignore the state of Christian mentalities conditioned by an anterior formation. This implies the research of a progressive pedagogy.

MANIPULATED MAN:
A SELECTED INTERNATIONAL BIBLIOGRAPHY
OF WORKS PUBLISHED SINCE 1970

It is impossible to present a bibliography which could include all aspects of the problem of the manipulation of man as there are so many areas in which this manipulation can be examined.

This bibliography is merely intended to bring together the different elements. From these it will be simple to further one's interests in any special area or to complete one's own documentation.

We have collected our material under two subjects:

I. *Manipulated Man* with a strong emphasis on bio-ethical problems.

II. *The Moral Norm* because this seems to be particularly involved in problems of the manipulation of man.

.

I. MANIPULATED MAN

Works on euthanasia and abortion often touch on our subject. So we have included several bibliographies on these
problems. However, we must emphasize that it is impossible
to present a complete bibliography on these subjects in the
present circumstances.

"Artificial insemination donor: a simple medical technique,
     a complex human problem", *Soundings*, 54 (1971), 288-343.

Barber, Bernard.   "Ethics of experimentation with human sub-
     jects", *Scientific American*, 234 (1976), 25-31.

_____. *Research on human subjects: problems of
     social control in medical experimentation.* New York:
     Russel Sage Foundation, 1973.

Bibliography of bioethics. Ed. by L. Walters. Vol. 1.
     Detroit: Gale Research Co., 1975.

"Bibliography of Joseph Fletcher. Publications: 1928-1977",
     Theology Today, 33 (1977), 409-422.

Bibliography of society, ethics and the life sciences. Comp.
     by S. Sollitto and R. M. Veatch. Hasting-on-Hudson:
     Hastings Center Publications, 1974.

*Die Biologische Zukunft des Menschen. Neun international
     bekannte Wissenschaftler nehmen Stellung zu den bren-
     nendsten Problemen unserer Zeit.* Frankfurt: Umschau-
     Verlag, 1971.

Biomedical ethics and the law. Ed. by J. M. Humber and R. E.
     Almeder. New York: Plenum Press, 1976.

"The biomedical revolution", *Engage/social action*, 1 (1973),
     6-63.

Böckle, Franz.   "Ethische Aspekte der Organtransplantation
     beim Menschen", *Studium generale*, 23 (1970), 444-459.

_____ et Eiff, A. W. von. "L'expérimentation dans la recherche clinique", *Concilium*, 65 (1971), 67-78.

Bone, Edouard. "Quelques thèmes actuels de bioéthique: manipulation de l'homme et expérimentation sur l'homme", *Revue théologique de Louvain*, 6 (1975), 412-437.

Boné, E. L. "La préoccupation bioéthique dans les pays anglo-saxons", *Revue théologique de Louvain*, 4 (1973), 340-356.

Breggin, Peter B. "Psychiatric totalitarianism. Nazi Germany and today", *Freedom*, 47 (1974), 6-7.

Callahan, D. J. "Bioethics as a discipline", *The Hastings Center Studies*, 1 (1973), 66-73.

Campbell, Alastair. *Moral dilemmas in medicine*. Baltimore: Williams and Wilkins, 1973.

Cauthen, Kenneth. *Christian biopolitics: a credo and strategy for the future*. Nashville: Abington, 1971.

The challenge of life. Biomedical progress and human values. Stuttgart: Birkhäuser Verlag, 1971.

"Chemie, Biologie und Ethik", *Zeitschrift für evangelische Ethik*, 16 (1972), 129-166.

Chiavacci, E. and Gedda, L. *Problemi morali manipolazione dell'uomo con particolare riguardo alla sperimentazione in embriologia*. Rome: Orizzonte Medico, 1970.

Comblin, Joseph. *Théologie de la pratique révolutionnaire* (Encyclopédie univ.). Paris: Edition universition, (1974), 381.

Coreth, E. "Freiheit und Bindung der Wissenschaft", *Zeitschrift für katholische Theologie*, 94 (1972), 129-144.

Crespy, G. "Biologie et théologie: interrogations et perspectives", *Foi et vie*, 6 (1972), 73-86.

Curran, Charles. "Human life", *Chicago studies*, 13 (1974), 292-295.

_____. "Moral theology and genetics", *Cross currents*, 20 (1970), 64-87.

_____. *Politics, medicine, and Christian ethics: a dialogue with Paul Ramsey*. Philadelphia: Fortress Press, 1973.

_____. "Theology and genetics: a multi-faceted dialogue", *Journal of ecumenical studies*, 7 (1970), 61-89.

David, G. and Czyglik, F. *et al.* "Nouvelles politiques en matière de don du sperme", in *Insémination artificielle et reproduction humaine*. Louvain: Centre International Cardinal Suenens, 1973, pp. 85-96.

De Souza, Eustace. "The ethics of human experimentation as viewed by a basic scientist", *Catholic medical quarterly*, 50 (1973), 173-177.

Dedek, John F. *Contemporary medical ethics*. New York: Sheed and Ward, 1975.

_____. "Remaking man", *Chicago studies*, 11 (Spring, 1972), 15-30.

_____. "Two moral cases: psychosurgery and behavior control; grossly malformed infants", *Chicago studies*, 14 (1975), 19-35.

Delepierre, A. "Réflexions éthiques sur les perspectives nouvelles en matière de reproduction humaine", in *Perspectives nouvelles en matières de reproduction humaine*. Louvain: Centre International Cardinal Suenens, 1973, pp. 22-47.

Den neuen Mensch planen. "Aspekte für die Zukunft aus der Biomedizin", *Evangelische Kommentare*, (1972), 260-265.

Desportes, J. P. "Les manipulations du comportement", *La Recherche*, 48 (1974), Special Issue.

Diamond, James J. "Abortion, animation and biological hominization", *Theological studies*, 36 (1975), 305-324.

Dierkens, R. "Les problèmes juridiques posés par l'insémination artificielle", in *Insémination artificielle et reproduction humaine*. Louvain: Centre International Cardinal Suenens, 1973, pp. 65-84.

Dobzhansky, T. G. "Ethics and values in biological and cultural evolution", *Zygon*, 8 (1973), 261-281.

Dumon, V. and Nijs, P. *et al.* "Donor insemination. A preliminary social and psychological report", in *Insemination artificielle et reproduction humaine*. Louvain: Centre International Cardinal Suenens, 1973, pp. 25-27.

Dyck, Arthur J. "Ethics and medicine", *Linacre quarterly*, 40 (1973), 182-200.

Eberhard, Kenneth D. "Genetics and human survival", *Linacre quarterly*, 40 (1973), 167-181.

Eckardt, Alice L. "The Holocaust: Christian and Jewish responses", *Journal of the American Academy of Religion*, 42 (1974), 453-469.

Elovitz, Mark H. "Bio-medical challenges to law and morality", *Judaism*, 24 (1975), 144-156.

Ethical and legal issues of social experimentation. Ed. by A. M. Rivlin and M. Timpane. Washington: Brookings Institute, 1976.

Ethical issues in human genetic counseling and the use of genetic knowledge. New York: Plenum, 1973.

"Ethics and human biology", *Humanist*, 32 (1972), 5-19.

Euthanasia/Euthanasie, in *RIC* 75, *RIC* 76, No. 240. Strasbourg: Cerdic Publications.

Failing, W. E. and May, H. *Mit Audiovisuellen Medien arbeiten*. Frankfurt am Main: Benzinger, 1975.

Férin, J. "Acquisitions récentes dans le domaine de la biologie nouvelle et de la reproduction humaine", in *Perspectives nouvelles en matière de reproduction humaine*. Louvain: Centre International Cardinal Suenens, 1973, pp. 2-21.

"Fetal research". Ed. by P. Steinfels, in *The Hastings center report*, 5 (1975), 11-46.

Fletcher, Joseph. "Ethical aspects of genetic controls", *New England journal of medicine*, 285 (1971), 776-783.

224

_____. "Ethical considerations in biomedical research involving human beings", in *International Conference on the Individual and Community*. Geneva: World Medical Society, 1976, pp. 121-142.

_____. *The Ethics of genetic control. Ending reproductive roulette*. New York: Doubleday, 1974.

_____. "Medicine, morals, religion", *Theology today*, 31 (1974), 39-46.

Fletcher, John. "Moral problems in genetic counseling", *Pastoral psychology*, 22 (1972), 47-60.

_____. "Realities of patient consent to medical research", *The Hastings center studies*, 1 (1973), 39-49.

_____. "The Promethean project and pastoral care", *Pastoral psychology*, 22 (1972), 7-14.

Floyd, Mary K. *Abortion bibliography*. Troy: Whitston Pub. Co., 1975.

Friedel, H. "Le néo-positivisme de Jacques Monod et l'idée qu'un biologiste chrétien peut se faire de la liberté", *Foi et vie*, 71 (1972), 51-70.

Garrett, Th. "Manipulation et mass media", *Concilium*, 65 (1971), 51-58.

"Genetic experimentation and the family", *Marriage and family living*, 57 (1975), 2-5.

"Genetics", *Theological studies*, 33 (1972), 401-552 (special issue).

Gill, David M. *From here to where? Technology, faith and the future of man*. Geneva: World Council of Churches, 1970.

Gritti, J. "Contraintes sociologiques et vie communautaire", *Le supplément*, 104 (1973), 94-111.

Guerin, Daniel. *Abortion/Avortement (1973-June 1975), (RIC suppl., 20)*. Strasbourg: Cerdic Publications, 1975.

Guild of Catholic doctors ethical committee, "In vitro fertilization", *Catholic medical quarterly*, 49 (1972), 237-243.

Guissard, Lucien. "Aspects éthiques des techniques d'information dans la presse", *Revue théologique de Louvain*, 6 (1975), 31-40.

Gustafson, James M. "Basic ethical issues in the biomedical fields", *Soundings*, 53 (1970), 151-180.

_____, Roblin, Richard, *et al.* "Ethical and social issues in screaming for genetic disease", *New England journal of medicine*, 286 (1972), 1129-1132.

Hamilton, Michael. *The new genetics and the future of man.* Grand Rapids: Eerdmans, 1973.

Hanink, J. G. "On the survival lottery", *Philosophy*, 50 (1975), 81-87; 51 (1975), 223-225.

Häring, Bernard. *Ethics of manipulation. Issues in medicine, behavior control and genetics.* New York: Seabury Press, 1975.

_____. *Heilender Dienst.* Mainz: Matthias Grünewald, 1972.

_____. *Manipulation. Ethical boundaries of medical behavioural and genetic manipulation.* Slough: St. Paul Publications, 1975.

_____. *Medical ethics.* Notre Dame: Fides, 1973.

Hatfield, Charles. *The scientist and ethical decision.* Downers Grove: Inter Varsity Press, 1973.

Heelan, P. A. "Nature and its transformations", *Theological studies*, 33 (1972), 486-502.

Hellegers, André E. "Some thoughts about medical problems for Catholics", *Chicago studies*, 1 (1972), 295-304.

Hilton, B. "The biomedical revolution", *Engage social action*, 1 (1973), 7-15.

Honecker, Martin. "Ethische Uberlegungen zur Dialyse und Transplantation", *Zeitschrift für evangelische Ethik,* 19 (1975), 129-142.

Huftier, M. "Le pouvoir de l'homme sur l'homme", *Esprit et vie,* 83 (1973), 681-688.

Human manipulation/Manipulation humaine, RIC 74, No. 295; *RIC* 75, No. 291; *RIC* 76, No. 291. Strasbourg: Cerdic Publications.

Illies, Joachim. *Für eine menschenwürdige Zukunft. Die gemeinsame Verantwortung von Biologie und Theologie.* Freiburg/Br.: Herder, 1972.

"In vitro fertilization", *Medical moral newsletter,* 8 (March-April, 1972), Special Issue.

Ingle, Dwight J. "Genetic bases of individuality and of social problems", *Zygon,* 61 (1971), 182-191.

Jacobs, William J. "The impending explosion in medical and bio-ethics", *Pastoral life,* (September, 1972), 25-30.

Joel, A. C. "Die therapeutische Insemination in heutiger Sicht", *Zeitschrift für evangelische Ethik,* 15 (1971), 215-226.

Kanoti, George A. "Surgical control of behavior", *Linacre quarterly,* 41 (1974), 193-199.

Kaplan, Morris B. "Case of the artificial heart panel", *The Hastings center report,* 5 (1975), 41-48.

Kass, Leon R. "Babies by means of in vitro fertilization: unethical experiments on the unborn?", *New England journal of medicine,* 285 (1971), 1174-1179.

_____. "Making babies--the new biology and the 'old' morality", *The public interest,* 8 (1972), 18-56.

_____. "The new biology: what price relieving man's estate", *Science,* 174 (1971), 779-788.

Keefe, Donald J. "Biblical symbolism and the morality of in vitro fertilization", *Theology digest,* 22 (1974), 308-323.

227

_____. "A review and critique of the CTSA report", *Hospital progress*, 54 (February, 1973), 57-69.

Knopp, Patricia. "Organ transplants are immoral", *U.S. Catholic*, 42 (1977), 12.

Krauss, Paul. *Medizinischer Fortschritt und ärztliche Ethik*. Münich: Beck Verlag, 1974.

Kunz, Robert M. and Fehr, Hans. *The challenge of life: bio-medical progress and human values*. Roche anniversary symposium, 1971. Basel: Birkhäuser, 1972.

Lewontin, R. C. "Biology and social problems", *Zygon*, 6 (1971), 192-194.

Linz, M. *Der veränderbare Mensch. Gespräche mit Humanwissenschaftlern*. Düsseldorf: Patmos, 1971.

Lobo, George V. *Current problems in medical ethics. A comprehensive guide to ethical problems in medical practice*. Allahabad: St. Paul Publications, 1974.

Luthe, H. O. "Qu'est-ce que la manipulation?", *Concilium*, 65 (1971), 13-26.

Lyons, Catherine. *Organ transplants*. London, SCM, 1971.

McCormick, R. A. "Genetic medicine: notes on the moral literature", *Theological studies*, 33 (1972), 531-552.

McCormick, Richard. "Institutional medico-moral responsibility", *Chicago studies*, 1 (1972), 305-314.

McCormick, Richard A. "Proxy consent in the experimentation situation", *Perspectives in biology and medicine*, 18 (1974), 2-20.

_____. "Questions in bioethics. Notes on moral theology, April-September 1974", *Theological studies*, 36 (1975), 117-129.

_____. "Transplantation of organs: a comment on Paul Ramsey", *Theological studies*, 36 (1975), 503-509.

McEnery, Gerald. "Genetic counseling", *Catholic medical quarterly*, 48 (October, 1971), 75-82.

McFaden, Charles J. *The dignity of life. Moral values in a changing society.* Huntington: Our Sunday Visitor, 1976.

Maclemore, Clinton W. *Clergyman's psychological handbook. Clinical information for pastoral counseling.* Grand Rapids: Eerdmans, 1974.

McMahon, Th. "Manipulation et biens de consommation", *Concilium*, 65 (1971), 79-86.

"The making of a person: the developmental years" (8 art.), *Social thought*, 2 (1976), 3-102.

Marston, R. Q. "Medical science, the clinical trial and society", *The Hastings center report*, 3 (1973), 1-4.

May, William E. "Biomedical technologies and ethics", *Chicago studies*, 1 (1972), 245-256.

_____. "Ethics and human identity. The challenge of the new biology", *Horizons*, 3 (1976), 17-37.

_____. "Experimenting on human subjects", *Linacre quarterly*, 41 (1974), 238-252.

Merks, K. W. "Cybernétique sociale ou éthique sociale. Réflexions sur la rationalité de l'agir humain", *Concilium*, 65 (1971), 37-50.

Mieth, Dietmar. "Manipulation und Sittlichkeit. Zum ersten Kongress europäischer Moraltheologen", *Herder Korrespondenz*, 27 (1973), 634-638.

Moltmann, J. "Hoffnung und die biomedizinische Zukunft des Menschen", *Evangelische Theologie*, 32 (1972), 309-326.

_____. "L'influence de l'homme et de la société sur le progrès biomédical", *Le supplément*, 108 (1974), 27-45.

Moral problems in medicine. Ed. by S. Gorovitz. Englewood Cliffs: Prentice-Hall, 1976.

Morals and medicine. New York: Oxford University Press, 1971.

Morison, R. S. and Twiss, S. B. "Human fetus as useful research material", *The Hastings center report*, 3 (1973), 8-10.

National Conference of Catholic Bishops, "U.S. medical directives", *Catholic mind*, 70 (1972), 56-61.

Nelson, James B. *Human medicine*. Minneapolis: Augsburg, 1974.

O'Donnell, Thomas. "Institutional medico-moral responsibility: a response to father McCormick", *Chicago studies*, 1 (1972), 315-318.

O'Donnel, Thomas J. *Medicine and Christian morality*. New York: Alba House, 1976.

Oosthuizen, G. C. *The ethics of tissues transplantation*. Cape Town: Timmins, 1973.

Oraison, Marc. *Implications psychologiques de l'insémination artificielle et reproduction humaine*. Louvain: Centre International Cardinal Suenens, 1973.

O'Rourke, Kevin. "An ethical evaluation of federal norms for fetal experimentation", *Linacre quarterly*, 43 (1976), 17-24.

Peter, W. G. "Ethical perspectives in the use of genetic knowledge", *Bio science*, 21 (1971), 1133-1137.

Pierre, P. "La stérilisation et la morale", *La pensée et les hommes*, 15 (1971), 43-47.

Pirard, Régnier and Pirard-Jennes, Josette. "A propos des greffes d'organes", *Revue théologique de Louvain*, 5 (1974), 442-453.

Potter, Rensselaer Van. *Bioethics: Bridge to the future*. Englewood Cliffs: Prentice Hall, 1971.

"Psychology-theology do they ever meet?" (3 art.), *Journal of the American scientific affiliation*, 27 (1975), 55-68.

Rahner, Karl. "A propos du problème de la manipulation génétique", *Ecrits théologiques*, 12 (1970), 77-120.

_____. "La manipulation de l'homme par l'homme", *Ecrits théologiques*, 12 (1970), 121-153.

Ramsey, Paul. *The fabricated man: the ethics of genetic control*. New Haven: Yale University Press, 1970.

Reback, Gary L. "Fetal experimentation. Moral, legal and medical implications", *Stanford law review*, 26 (1974), 1191-1227.

Reick, Warren T. "Medical ethics: the contemporary context", *Chicago studies*, 1 (1972), 279-294.

Reiser, William. "Ethics and the biological man: an essay on ethical method", *Studies in religion*, 2 (1972), 50-62.

Religious systems and psychotherapy. Ed. by R. H. Cox. Springfield: C. Thomas, 1973.

Rizzo, Robert and Yonder, Joseph. "Care of the dying: the doctor and euthanasia", *Linacre quarterly*, 41 (1974), 253-268.

Robert, Charles. "Deux congrès de théologie morale", *Revue théologique de Louvain*, 3 (1972), 228-239.

Rogers, C. "Biomedics, psychosurgery and laissez-faire", *Christian century*, 90 (1973), 1076-1078.

Rorvik, David M. *Brave new baby: promise and peril of the biological revolution*. Garden City: Doubleday, 1971.

Rotter, Hans. "Die Manipulation des Menschen", *Arzt und Christ*, (1970), 21-29.

Ruff, W. *Organverpflanzung. Ethische Probleme aus katholisher Sicht*. München: Goldmann, 1971.

Schoysman, R. and Schoysman-Deboeck, A. "Expérience d'insémination artificielle par donneur. Résultats sur 205 grossesses", in *Insemination artificielle et reproduction humaine*. Louvain: Centre International Cardinal Suenens, 1973, pp. 7-24.

Sernett, Milton. "The 'death with dignity' debate: why we care", *The Springfielder*, 38 (1975), 265-277.

Simon, René. "Expérimentations et déplacements éthiques. A propos de l'insémination artificielle", *Recherches de science religieuse*, 62 (1974), 515-539.

Smith, Harman L. "Genetics and ethics: reaffirming the tragic vision", *Linacre quarterly*, 40 (1973), 158-166.

Sporken, Paul. "Braucht die Medizin eine neue Ethik", *Arzt und Christ*, (1973), 90-99.

_____. *Darf die Medizin, was sie kann? Problem der medizinischen Ethik*. Düsseldorf: Patmos, 1971.

Springer, R. H. "Notes on moral theology: September 1970-March 1971", *Theological studies*, 32 (1971), 465-488.

Steinfels, Peter. "Against bioethicists", *The Hastings center report*, 6 (1976), 18-19.

Stinson, Charles. "Theology and the Baron Frankenstein: clouing and beyond", *Christian century*, 89 (1972), 60-63.

Thielen, P. "Morale et biologie. Réticences d'un biologiste", *Bulletin de l'union catholique des scientifiques français*, 126 (1972), 5-12.

Timaens, Ernst. *Experiment und Psychologie. Zur Sozialpsychologie psychologischen Experimentierens*. Göttingen: Hogrefe, 1974.

Troisfontaine, R. "L'insémination artificielle. Problèmes éthiques", in *Insemination artificielle et reproduction humaine*. Louvain: Centre International Cardinal Suenens, 1973, pp. 97-132.

Vaux, Kenneth. "Cyborg, R. U. Human? Ethical issues in rebuilding man", *Religion in life*, 39 (1970), 187-192.

Veatch, R. M. "Does ethics have an empirical basis?", *The Hastings center studies*, 1 (1973), 50-65.

_____. "Generalization of expertise", *The Hastings center studies*, 1 (1973), 29-40.

_____. "Human experimentation committees. Professional or representative", *The Hastings center report*, 5 (1975), 31-40.

_____. "Medical ethics: professional or universal", *Harvard theological review*, 65 (1972), 531-560.

_____. "Medical model; its nature and problems", *The Hastings center studies*, 1 (1973), 59-76.

_____ and Sollitto, Sharman. "Human experimentation; the ethical questions persist", *The Hastings center report*, 3 (1973), 1-3.

Visscher, Maurice B. *Humanistic perspectives in medical ethics*. Amherst: Prometheus Books, 1973.

Vodopivek, M. "Eine pastoralmedizinische Anmerkung zum Problem der Humanontogenese", *Theologische Quartalschrift*, 151 (1971), 222-227.

Wagner, F. *Menschenzüchtung. Das Problem der genetischen Manipulierung des Menschen*. Münich: Beck, 1969.

Walters, Leroy. "Ethical issues in experimentation on the human fetus", *The journal of religious ethics*, 2 (1974), 22-75.

_____. "Genetic science and man: nine variations on a bioethical theme", *Linacre quarterly*, 39 (1972), 223-231.

_____ and Gaylin, Willard. "Sterilizing the retarded child", *The Hastings center report*, 6 (1976), 13-15.

_____. "Technology assessment and genetics", *Theological studies*, 33 (1972), 666-683.

Warren, M. A. "On the moral and legal status of abortion", *The monist*, 57 (1973), 43-61.

Webb, Benedict. "In vitro fertilization of human ova or test-tube babies", *Catholic medical quarterly*, 48 (1971), 69-75.

Weizsäcker, Ernst von. "Ethische Probleme aus der Biologie", *Zeitschrift für evangelische Ethik*, 16 (1972), 150-157.

_____. "The hopes of a scientific age", *Anticipation*, 3 (1970), 3-7.

Wenzmer, C. "Darf die menschliche Erbmasse künstlich verändert werden?", *Wege zum Menschen*, 22 (1970), 76-78.

Westerbarkey, Joachim. "'Manipulation' und kein Ende?--Ein Plädoyer für die Entwicklung einer kommunikations-politischen Gesamtkonzeption", *Communicatio socialis*, 7 (1974), 312-319.

Wilfried, Ruff. *Organverpflanzung: ethische Probleme aus katholischer Sicht*. München: Goldmann, 1971.

234

II. THE MORAL NORM

Allard, Henry. "The question of moral absolutes", *Theology*, 75 (1972), 232-237.

Anderson, J. N. D. *Morality, law and grace.* London: Tyndale, 1972.

Aubert, J. M. "Pour une herméneutique du droit naturel", *Recherche de science religieuse,* 59 (1971), 449-492.

Auer, Alfons. *Autonome Moral und christlicher Glaube.* Düsseldorf: Patmos, 1971.

_____. "Die Seite der Herausgeber", *Theologische Quartalschrift,* 155 (1975), 331-332.

Aultman, M. H. "Toward a new basis for law", *Lutheran quarterly,* 23 (1971), 223-230.

Balthasar, Hans U. von. "Commission théologique internationale. Pour situer la morale chrétienne", *La Documentation catholique,* 72 (1975), 420-426.

Beck, Horst W. von. "Denken und Entscheiden im kybernetischen Modell. Eine kritische Stellungnahme zum Thema 'Theologie und Empirie'", *Zeitschrift für evangelische Ethik,* 18 (1974), 225-245.

_____. "Wahrheit und Geschichte. Zur Frage der Absolutheit oder Relativität ethischer Werte und Normen. Bibliographie", *Salzburger Jahrbuch für Philosophie,* 14 (1970, 1971), 253-271.

Böckle, Franz. "Die Frage der Unfehlbarkeit sittlicher Normen", *Schweizerische Kirchenzeitung,* 143 (1975), 65-68.

_____. "La morale fondamentale", *Recherches de science religieuse,* 59 (1971), 331-364.

Bockmühl, Klaus. "Sens et non-sens de la nouvelle morale. Critique et auto-critique", *La revue réformée,* 26 (1975), 1-24.

Bönisch, Siegfried and Noack, Klaus-P. "Zu einigen Unterschieden zwischen moralischen Normen. Werturteilen und Aussagen", *Deutsche Zeitschrift für Philosophie*, 23 (1975), 818-829.

Boyd, Malcolm. "Law. Sacred writ or institutionalized injustice?", *Christian century*, 93 (1976), 592-596.

Brugger, Walter. "Bemerkungen zur Unveränderlichkeit und Veränderlichkeit der menschlichen Natur und des Sittengesetzes", *Theologie und Philosophie*, 46 (1971), 554-556.

Carlson, John. "Three levels of discussion about abortion", *Dimension*, 8 (1976), 37-45.

Chazan, Barry. "Who is moral man", *Religious education*, 71 (1976), 27-39.

Connolly, Thomas. "Morality and law", *Australian catholic record*, (1971), 310-333.

Cooper, Eugen. "Kurzformeln der Moral: zu den Grundnormen einer 'neuen' Moral", *Neue Ordnung*, (1972), 413-425.

Coreth, E. "Freiheit und Bindung der Wissenschaft", *Zeitschrift für katholische Theologie*, 94 (1972), 129-144.

Curran, Charles. "How my mind has changed: 1960-1975", *Horizons*, 2 (1975), 187-205.

_____. "Moral theology: the present state of the discipline", *Theological studies*, 34 (1973), 446-467.

Delhaye, Philippe. "Le légal n'est pas le moral", *Esprit et vie*, 87 (1977), 74-75.

_____. "L'objectivité en morale", *Esprit et vie*, 84 (1974), 369-380; 386-392.

_____. "Les récentes directives pontificales concernant l'enseignement de la théologie morale", *Revue théologique de Louvain*, 7 (1976), 456-468.

_____. "Réflexions sur la loi et les lois dans la vie de l'église", *L'Année canonique*, 18 (1974), 67-93.

_____. "Unité et diversité en morale", *Esprit et vie*, 83 (1973), 322-328; 337-342.

Delhaye, Philippe and Schürmann, Heinz. "Commission théologique internationale: l'impact actuel des normes morales du nouveau testament", *Esprit et vie*, 85 (1975), 593-603.

_____. "L'impact des normes morales du nouveau testament sur la vie chrétienne", *La documentation catholique*, 72 (1975), 761-766.

Demmer, Klaus. "Moralische Norm und theologische Anthropologie", *Gregorianum*, 54 (1973), 263-306.

_____. *Sein und Gebot. Die Bedeutsamkeit des transzendentalphilosophischen Denkansatzes in der Scholastik der Gegenwart für den formalen Aufriss der Fundamentalmoral.* Vienna: Paderborn, Schöningh, 1971.

_____. "Das Verhältnis von Recht und Moral im Licht kirchlicher Dispenspraxis", *Gregorianum*, 56 (1975), 681-731.

Díez-Alegría, J. M. "Manipulation et liberté dans l'Église *Concilium*, 65 (1971), 59-66.

"Discerner les valeurs pour fonder la morale" (9 art.), *Concilium*, 120 (1976), 7-140.

"Droit, moeurs, morale" (6 art.), *Le Supplément*, 115 (1975), 381-468.

Dubay, Thomas. "The state of moral theology", *Theological studies*, 35 (1974), 482-506.

Ermecke, Gustav. "Absolutes und Relatives im christlichen Denken und Leben nach katholischer Lehre", *Catholica*, 25 (1971), 198-213.

_____. "Christlichkeit und Geschichtlichkeit der Moraltheologie", *Catholica*, 26 (1972), 193-211.

_____. "Krise der Moral, Krise der Moraltheologie", *Theologie und Glaube*, 64 (1974), 338-356.

"Ethics and mysticism" (3 art.), *The Journal of religious ethics*, 4 (1976), 3-46.

Euthanasie. Hrsg. von H.-D. Hiersche. München: R. Piper, 1975.

Finance, Joseph de. "La détermination de la norme morale. Quelques réflexions", *Gregorianum*, 57 (1976), 703-740.

Fischer, G. R. "Search for ethics", *Ethics*, 81 (1971), 260-270.

Fleckenstein, Heinz. "Sittliche Normen christlicher Sexualerziehung in Schule und Elternhaus", *Anzeiger für die katholische Geistlichkeit*, 85 (1976), 421-422.

Fraling, Bernhard. "Glaube und Ethos: Normfindung in der Gemeinschaft der Gläubigen", *Theologie und Glaube*, 63 (1973), 81-104.

_____. "Normenbegründung in der Diskussion", *Theologie und Glaube*, 64 (1974), 389-400.

Frey, Christofer, "Zwischen Intuition und goldener Regel", *Zeitschrift für evangelische Ethik*, 19 (1975), 215-233.

Friedrichs, Robert W. "Social research and theology: end of the detente?", *Review of religious research*, 15 (1974), 113-127.

Fuchs, Josef. "Der Absolutheitscharakter sittlicher Handlungsnormen", in Wolter, H., *Testimonium veritati*. Frankfurt: *Frankfurter theologische Studien*, 1971, pp. 211-240.

_____. *Existe-t-il une "morale chretienne"?* Gembloux: Duculot, 1973.

_____. "Sittliche Normen. Universalien und Generalisierungen", *Münchener theologische Zeitschrift*, 25 (1974), 18-33.

_____. "The absoluteness of moral terms", *Gregoranium*, 52 (1971), 418-422.

238

Garceau, B. "La théologie transcendentale et son interprétation de l'histoire. A propos d'un livre de J. B. Metz", *Eglise et théologie*, 1 (1970), 375-393.

Genewein, Curt M. and Sporken, Paul. *Menschlich pflegen*. Düsseldorf: Patmos, 1975.

Ginters, Rudolf. *Die Ausdruckshandlung. Eine Untersuchung inrer sittlichen Bedeutsamkeit* (Moraltheol Studien. Systematische Abteilung, 4). Düsseldorf: Patmos, 1976.

_____. *Typen ethischer Argumentation. Zur Begründung sittlicher Normen.* Düsseldorf: Patmos, 1976.

Grant, M. Colin. "Revealing analogies in recent theology", *Studies in religion*, 4 (1974/75), 31-36.

Gründel, Johannes. "Kann die Moraltheologie von der Verhaltensforschung lernen?", *Entschluss*, 9 (1975), 453-457.

_____. *Peut-on changer la morale?* Paris: Cerf-Desclée, 1973.

_____. *Wandelbares und Unwandelbares in der Moraltheologie. Erwägungen zur Moraltheologie an Hand des Axioms "agere sequitur esse".* Düsseldorf: Patmos, 1971.

Gustafson, James M. "What is the normatively human?", *The American ecclesiastical review*, 165 (1971), 192-207.

Hanus, J. G. "Natural law--indispensable or not?", *The American Benedictine review*, 23 (1972), 85-97.

Häring, Bernhard. *Sünde im Zeitalter der Säkularisation.* Graz: Styria, 1974.

_____. *Une morale pour la personne.* Paris: Mame, 1973.

Hauerwas, Stanley. *Character and the Christian life: a study in theological ethics.* San Antonio: Trinity University Press, 1975.

Herr, Theodor. "Perspectiven eines dynamisch-geschichtlichen, biblisch-eschatologischen Naturrechtes", *Jahrbuch für christliche Sozialwissenschaften*, 13 (1972), 111-135.

_____. *Zur Frage nach dem Naturrecht im deutschen Protestantismus der Gegenwart*. Munich: Schöningh, 1972.

Holmes, Arthur F. "The concept of natural law", *Christian scholar's review*, 2 (1972), 195-208.

Hörmann, Karl. "Die Bedeutung der konkreten Wirklichkeit für das sittliche Tun nach Thomas von Aquin", *Theologisch-praktische Quartalschrift*, 123 (1975), 118-129.

Huftier, M. "Conscience individuelle et règle morale", *Esprit et vie*, 85 (1975), 465-476; 481-489.

Hughes, G. J. "A Christian basis for ethics", *Heythrop journal*, 13 (1972), 242-257.

Hurley, Neil P. "The natural law and man's 'open-ended' nature", *New Catholic world*, 216 (1973), 259-263.

Huth, Werner. "Abbau von Zwängen im kirchlichen Raum?", *Stimmen der Zeit*, 100 (1975), 736-744.

Jackson, John S. "Shall we legislate morality?", *Review and expositor*, 73 (1976), 173-177.

Jeffko, Walter G. "Processive relationism and ethical absolutes", *American Benedictine review*, 26 (1975), 283-297.

Kaufman, G. D. "A problem for theology: the concept of nature", *Harvard theological review*, 65 (1972), 337-366.

Kerber, Walter. "Christliche Normen im Rechtsbereich?", *Stimmen der Zeit*, 192 (1974), 241-255.

_____. "Hermeneutik in der Moraltheologie", *Theologie und Philosophie*, 44 (1969), 42-66.

Knauer, Peter. "Überlegungen zur moraltheologischen Prinzipienlehre der Enzyklika 'Humanae vitae'", *Theologie und Philosophie*, 45 (1970), 60-74.

Korff, Wilhelm. *Norm und Sittlichkeit, Untersuchungen zur Logik der normativen Vernunft*. Mainz: Matthias Grünewald, 1973.

Kühn, Ulrich. "Evangelische Anmerkungen zum Problem der Begründung der moralischen Autonomie des Menschen im neuen Gesetz nach Thomas", *Angelicum*, 51 (1974), 235-245.

Leclercq, Georges, "Y a-t-il une loi morale chrétienne", *Mélanges de science religieuse*, 32 (1975), 177-192.

Lester, William. *Morality, anyone?* New Rochelle: Arlington H., 1975.

Lewis, Tom T. "What is the ultimate basis of human morality?", *Religious humanism*, 10 (1976), 87-91.

"Liberté et contrainte sexuelle" (11 art.), *Parole et société*, 83 (1975), 427-513.

"Loi naturelle et droit naturel", *Chronique sociale de France*, (September, 1971), 3-97.

Love and society. Essays in the ethics of Paul Ramsey. Ed. by J. Johnson and D. Smith. (JRE studies in religious ethics, 1) Tallahassee: Scholars Press, 1975.

Loving women/loving men; gay liberation and the church. Ed. by S. Gearhart and W. R. Johnson. San Francisco: Clide, 1974.

McCormick, Richard A. "Notes on moral theology", *Theological studies*, 35 (1974), 312-359.

——————————————. "Transplantation of organs: a comment on Paul Ramsey", *Theological studies*, 36 (1975), 503-509.

Mehl, Roger. "Universalité ou particularité du discours de la théologie morale", *Recherches de science religieuse*, 59 (1971), 365-384.

Milhaven, John Giles. "Objective moral evaluation of consequences", *Theological studies*, 32 (1971), 407-430.

Moingt, Joseph. "Le dieu de la morale chrétienne", *Recherches de science religieuse*, 62 (1974), 631-654.

Montagnes, B. "Autonomie et dignité de l'homme", *Angelicum*, 51 (1974), 186-211.

Morals norm/Morale norme. Strasbourg: Cerdic-Publications, Ric 76, No. 462.

Mpongo, Mpoto M. "Le critère de moralité dans l'éthique sexuelle des Ntómba", *Telema*, 2 (1976), 53-58.

Munk, Hans J. "Moralische Normen, theologische Gewissheit und Humanwissenschaften", *Trierer theologische Zeitschrift*, 85 (1976), 362-373.

Newman, Jeremiah. *Conscience versus law; reflections on the revolution of natural law*. Chicago: Franciscan Herald Press, 1972.

"Normen im Wandel" (3 art.), *Entschluss*, 5 (1976), 225-238.

O'Callaghan, Denis. "What has happened to the ten commandments?", *Furrow*, 26 (1975), 36-42.

O'Biordan, Sean. "The teaching of the papal encyclicals as source and norm of moral theology: a historical and analytic survey", *Studia moralia*, 14 (1976), 135-157.

O'Connel, Timothy E. "The question of moral norms", *American ecclesiastical review*, 169 (1975), 377-388.

Pancovski, I. "Die Entwicklung des orthodoxen ethischen Denkens in den sozialistischen Ländern Osteuropas", *Ostkirchliche Studien*, 25 (1976), 303-320.

Perkins, Lisa H. "Natural law in contemporary analytic philosophy", *American journal of jurisprudence*, 17 (1972), 111-119.

Pohier, J. M. *Le chrétien, le plaisir et la sexualité* (Foi vivante). Paris: Cerf, 1974.

Price, Richard. *A review of the principal questions in morals*. Oxford: Oxford University Press, 1974.

"Das Problem der Normfindung", *Religionsunterricht an höheren Schulen*, 17 (1974), 162-200.

Puza, Richard. "Die Prüfung fehlerhafter Gesetze im Kirchen-
    recht--ein Beitrag zum Problem der Normenkontrolle",
    Oesterreichiches Archiv für Kirchenrecht, 26 (1975),
    90-119.

Rae, S. H. "Regel und Kontext in der gegenwärtigen christ-
    lichen Ethik", *Zeitschrift für evangelische Ethik*, 16
    (1972), 357-367.

Read, D. "The great debate: natural law theories and/or
    human wisdom", *The American ecclesiastical review*,
    165 (1971), 187-191.

Religion und Moral. Hrsg. von B. Gladigow. Düsseldorf:
    Patmos, 1976.

Remy, P. *Foi chrétienne et morale*. Paris: Le Centurion,
    1973.

"Responses to lifeboat ethics discussion" (2 art.), *Sound-
    ings*, 59 (1976), 234-249.

Rich, Arthur. "Die theologische Sozialethik vor dem Umwelts-
    problem", *Reformatio*, 23 (1974), 551-564.

Ricken, Friedo. "Die Begründung moralischer Urteile nach R.
    M. Hare", *Theologie und Philosophie*, 51 (1976), 344-
    358.

Robert, Charles. "Le légal et le moral", *La Documentation
    Catholique*, 71 (1974), 883-890.

_____. "La situation de 'conflit', un thème dan-
    gereux de la théologie morale aujourd'hui", *Revue des
    sciences religieuses*, 44 (1970), 190-213.

Robinson, N. H. G. *The groundwork of Christian ethics*.
    Grand Rapids: Eerdmans, 1972.

Rosset, Clément. *L'anti-nature*. Paris: P.U.F., 1973.

Rotter, H. "Die Eigenart der christlichen Ethik", *Stimmen
    der Zeit*, 102 (1973), 407-416.

_____. "Grundlagen der Moral. Uberlegungen zu einer
    moraltheologischen Hermeneutik", *Theologische Berichte*,
    4 (1975), 7-171.

_____. *Grundlagen der Moral. Überlegungen zu einer moraltheologischen Hermeneutik* (Theologische Berichte, 4). Zurich: Benzinger, 1975.

_____. "Kann das Naturrecht die Moraltheologie entbehren", *Zeitschrift für katholische Theologie*, 96 (1974), 76-96.

_____. "Zur Grundlegung einer christlichen Sexualethik", *Stimmen der Zeit*, 100 (1975), 115-125.

Ruf, A. K. *Grundkurs: Moraltheologie. 1 Gesetz und Norm.* Freiburg: Herder, 1975.

Sagne, J. C. "La loi, la réciprocité et le don", *Le Supplément*, 108 (1974), 3-26.

Schall, James V. *Human dignity and human numbers.* Staten Island: Alba House, 1971.

Schmitz, Philipp. *Die Wirklichkeit fassen: zur "induktiven" Normenfassung einer "neuer Moral".* Frankfurt: Knecht, 1972.

Schueller, Bruno. *Die Begründung ethischer Urteile. Typen ethischer Argumentation in der katholischen Moraltheologie.* Düsseldorf: Patmos, 1973.

_____. "Zum Problem ethischer Normierung", *Orientierung*, (1972), 81-84.

_____. "Zur Problematik allgemein verbindlicher ethischer Grundsätze", *Theologie und Philosophie*, 45 (1970), 1-23.

_____. "Zur Rede von der radikalen sittlichen Forderung", *Theologie und Philosophie*, 46 (1971), 321-341.

Scholz, Franz. "Durch ethische Grenzsituationen aufgeworfene Normenprobleme. Ansätze zur Lösung bei Thomas V. A. und bei Bonaventura", *Theologischpraktische Quartalschrift*, 123 (1975), 341-355.

_____. *Wege, Umwege und Auswege der Moraltheologie. Ein Plädoyer für begründete Ausnahmen.* München: Don Bosco, 1976.

244

Schüller, Bruno. "Neuere Beiträge zum Thema Begründung sittlicher Normen", *Theologische Berichte*, 4 (1974), 109-181.

Schultze, H. "Ueberlegungen zu einer zukunftsorientierten Ethik", *Zeitschrift für evangelische Ethik*, 16 (1972), 257-272.

Schürmann, Heinz. "Haben die Paulinischen Wertungen und Weisungen Modellcharakter?", *Gregorianum*, 56 (1975), 237-271.

Seckler, Max. "Zur Diskussion um die Grundwerte in Staat und Gesellschaft", *Theologische Quartalschrift*, 156 (1976), 316-318.

Sherman, Frank. "A new ethic for a new age?", *Dialog*, 14 (1975), 33-37.

Simon, René. *Fonder la morale. Dialectique de la foi et de la raison pratique*. Paris: Seuil, 1974.

_____. "Situation de l'éthique dans l'existence chrétienne", *Lumière et vie*, 23 (1974), 83-97.

Spae, Joseph J. "Le climat de la théologie au Japon", *Revue théologique de Louvain*, 7 (1976), 171-181.

Stackhouse, Max L. "The location of the holy", *The Journal of religious ethics*, 4 (1976), 63-104.

Stanton, Michael. "The assessment of moral judgments: cultural and cognitive considerations", *Religious education*, 71 (1976), 610-621.

Sterns, J. Brenton. "Normative theology and metaphysics", *Studies in religion*, 4 (1974/75), 37-44.

Stoeckle, Bernard. "Das Problem der sittlichen Norm", *Stimmen der Zeit*, 100 (1975), 723-735.

_____. *Grenzen der Autonomen Moral*. München: Kösel, 1974.

Sublon, Roland. "Crise des normes", *Concilium*, 114 (1976), 89-96.

245

Szczesny, Gerhard. *Das sogenannte Gute. Vom Unvermögen der Ideologen*. Reinbeck b/Hamburg: Rowohlt, 1971.

Thibaud, Tancrède. "La bible dans le droit français", *Conscience et liberté*, 9 (1975), 40-46.

Thielicke, Helmut. "Anthropologische Grundbestände in individuellen Konfliktsituationen", *Zeitschrift für evangelische Ethik*, 18 (1974), 129-145.

_____. *Mensch sein--Mensch werden. Entwurf einer christlichen Anthropologie*. München: Piper, 1976.

Thompson, Kenneth W. "Right and wrong. A framework for moral reasoning", *Christian century*, 92 (1975), 705-708.

Tracy, David. "La dimension religieuse de la science", *Concilium*, 81 (1973), 127-134.

Vallery, Jacques. *L'identité de la morale chrétienne. Points de vue de quelques théologiens contemporains de langue allemande*. Louvain: Univ. cath., 1975. (Thèse doctorat en theol.)

Veatch, Henry B. *For an ontology of morals: a critique of contemporary ethical theory*. Evanston: Northwestern University Press, 1971.

Verdross, A. *Statisches und dynamisches Naturrecht*. Freiburg: Rombach, 1970.

"Virtue and obligation in religious ethics", *The Journal of religious ethics*, 1 (1973), 5-63.

Virtus politica. Festgabe zum 75. Geburtstag von Alfons Hufnagel. Stuttgart: Frommann Friedrich Vlg., 1974.

Vohn, Josef. *Sittliche erkenntnis zwischen Rationalität und Glauben. Ein aspekt der säkularisierung im licht der theologie Friedrich Gogartens*. Paderborn: Bonifacius, 1977.

"Wie kommt es zu ethischen Imperativen? Sprachphilosophische Ansätze zur Begründung von Normen", *Evangelische Kommentare*, (1972), 452-456.

Winters, Francis X. *Politics and ethics: patterns in partnership*. New York: Paulist Press, 1975.

M. Zimmermann

CONTRIBUTORS

Jacques Audinet. Director of the Institut Supérieur de Pastorale Catéchétique de Paris.

Franz Böckle. Professor of moral theology at the University of Bonn.

J. Férin. Professor at the Université de Louvain. Director of the University Maternity.

Jules Gritti. Professor of sociology at the Institut Catholique de Paris.

Joachim Illies. Professor of zoology at the University of Giessen. Director of Max-Plauck-Institute of Schlitz Hessen.

Wilhelm Korff. Professor of moral theology at the Tübingen University.

Maurice Nédoncelle. The late Honorary Dean and Professor at the Faculté de théologie Catholique de l'Université des Sciences humaines de Strasbourg.

Charles Robert. Honorary professor at the Faculté de theologie Catholique de Strasbourg.

Heinrich Rombach. Professor of philosophy at the University of Würzburg.

Br. Schüller. University of Bochum.

Roland Sublon. Doctor of Medicine and Theology. Dean of the Faculté de théologie Catholique de l'Université des Sciences humaines de Strasbourg.

Marie Zimmermann. Researcher at Cerdic.